101 Gluten Free Indian Recipes

By Shelina Mann

Indian Cooking Delights Series

All contents copyrighted © 2014 by Shelina Mann. All rights reserved worldwide. No part of this document or the related materials may be reproduced or transmitted in any form, by any means (electronic, photocopying, recording, or otherwise) without the prior permission by the author/publisher.

The recipes contained within the 101 Gluten Free Indian Recipes are based on the author's research. The research has been done through credible sources to the best of our knowledge. Many of these recipes have been tried and tasted many times over, to bring you the most tasty of Indian Gluten Free Recipes.

In no event shall the author be liable for any direct, indirect, incidental, punitive, or consequential damages of any kind whatsoever with respect to the service, the materials and the products contained within. This book is not intended to be a substitute to professional culinary advice.

Contents

INTRODUCTION 7
SPICES AND INGREDIENTS 11
    Basic Chicken Stock 12
    Basic Vegetable Stock 13
    Temperature Guide 14
APPETIZERS 15
    Paneer Masala 16
    Chick Pea Fritters 18
    Vegetable Pakora 19
    Papri Chat 20
    Chicken Pakora 22
    Potato & Spinach Pies 24
    Lamb Meatballs 26
    Potato Fritters 27
    Onion Fritters 28
    Cassava Chips 29
    Fish Pakoras 30
    Kachoris 31
    Chicken Kofta 33
    Onion & Rice Bhajis 34
    Carrot Dosai 35
CHUTNEYS/SAUCES 37
    Raita 38
    Roasted Garlic Raita 39
    Mint Sauce 40
    Tomato & Ginger Chutney 41
    Apple Chutney 42
    Coriander Chutney 43
    Tamarind Chutney 44
    Coconut Chutney 45
    Red Chili Chutney 46
    Curried Onion Chutney 47
    Mango Pickle 48
    Carrot Pickle 49
SALADS/ SOUPS 51
    Sweet Potato Soup 52
    Carrot & Beetroot Soup 54

Sweet Corn and Chicken Soup 55
Tomato Soup 57
Spinach Soup 59
Pepper Rasam 60
Bean Salad 62
Vegetable Salad 63
Punjabi Salad 64
Onion/Tomato Salad 65

VEGETABLE AND LENTIL CURRIES 67

Red Chori Lentil Curry 68
Yellow Curry with Cauliflower and Squash 70
Green Curry with Sweet Potatoes and Peppers 71
Roasted Root Vegetable Curry 74
Plaintain Tomato Kofta 75
Paneer & Green Pea Curry 77
Masala Green Beans 79
Split Yellow Dhal 80
Chickpea Dhal 81
Black Eye Beans 82
Potato with Cauliflower 83
Spinach Saag 84
Carrots Peas & Potatoes 85
Eggplant 86
Okra 87
Spinach with Paneer 88
Red Kidney Beans 89

SNACKS 91

Bhel Puri 92
Spicy Gluten Free Crackers 93
Sabudana Vada 94
Poppadums 95
Bhakri 96
Spiced Nut Mix 97
Lentil Spread 98

FISH AND SEAFOOD 99

Spicy Coconut Shrimp 100
Fish Cakes 101
Shrimp Balchao 103
Curried Halibut 104
Fish with Red Curry 105

  Tandoori Fish *106*
  Fish & Tomato Curry *107*
  Coconut Lime Fish *108*

EGG, CHICKEN AND LAMB 109

  Egg Masala with Potatoes *110*
  Curried Eggs with Raita *111*
  Eggs Poached in Tomato Chili Sauce *112*
  Chick Peas and Spinach with Chicken *113*
  Chicken with Cardamom *115*
  Roasted Chicken *116*
  Butter Chicken *117*
  Fried Chicken Masala *119*
  Tandoori Chicken *120*
  Chicken Coriander *122*
  Lamb Haleem *123*
  Lamb Gosht *125*
  Tandoori Lamb *127*

ROTI, NANS, PARATHA AND TEPLAS 129

  Gluten Free Roti *130*
  Savory Gluten Free Paratha *131*
  Gluten Free Methi Teplas *132*
  Sweet Gluten Free Naan with Raisins & Nuts *133*
  Cauliflower Stuffed Paratha *134*

RICE 137

  Vegetable Biryana *138*
  Jeera Rice *140*
  Chicken Biryana *141*
  Peas Pillau *143*
  Sweet Rice with Raisins and Nuts *144*
  Carrot Rice *145*

DESSERTS 147

  Pistachio Kulfi *148*
  Gulab Jambu *149*
  Mango Lassi *151*
  Carrot Halwa *152*
  Coconut Barfi *153*
  Plain Sweet Lassi *154*

Introduction

Indian cuisine is perfect for people on a gluten-free diet. In India food is regarded as medicine, and meals are made according to Ayurvedic principles. The centuries old practice of Ayurvedic Medicine treats many illnesses before they become chronic by choosing foods that balance the body and allow the body to rest and heal itself. Ayurveda (recently popular in the West) focuses on creating harmony within the body and by creating a natural relationship with the environment. Ayurveda acknowledges different doshas (constitutions) and has recommended diets to bring the dosha into balance. This concept is vital to people on a gluten-free diet to ensure that they preserve their good health and maintain a good quality of life.

If you're starting a gluten-free diet, you are beginning a very challenging diet. Gluten appears in many foods, including foods you would not expect. It is important that you know what you can and cannot eat to maintain a gluten-free diet. If you are eating a gluten free diet for celiac disease even small amounts of gluten can cause the body's immune system to attack and damage the small intestine, causing pain, discomfort and long term health problems.

Gluten is the protein in grains and grasses, almost all grains and grasses have gluten. However all gluten is not the same. The gluten that people with celiac disease and gluten intolerance must avoid is the gluten in a specific group of sub-grains from the Pooideae subfamily of the Poaceae family of grasses. The Poaceae family represents over ten thousand species of grasses, including bamboo and corn. It is an important modern crop for food, materials and fuel. The sub-grains from the Pooideae family include wheat, barley, rye and oats. For those suffering from celiac disease the gluten in rice and corn is safe to eat, however the gluten in wheat, barley or rye is not. Knowing what foods are safe to eat can make eating a gluten free diet more easier and enjoyable. Many people who do not have celiac disease suffer from gluten intolerance or are gluten sensitive, they can experience many of the same symptoms as people with celiac disease. (Oats are borderline for gluten, so people are fine others will struggle with eating it.)

Learning how to eat a gluten-free diet is difficult, you have to give up many of the staples of a normal diet. If you don't know all of the ingredients in a dish or food product, to protect your health, you probably should not eat it. You have to learn a new way to plan your meals, how to shop, how to prepare your meals and how to dine out.

As gluten can be found in so many foods that you do not expect you have to be knowledgeable about what you can and cannot eat. Eating safely on a gluten free diet can be frustrating, but it can be done. You can make and eat delicious tasting and healthy meals for yourself, your family and friends; that are gluten-free and no one will know the difference.

With a long history, India has had many influences over thousands of years, to develop culinary traditions. There are many different styles of foods to choose from, so you have a large variety of foods that are sweet, savory, spicy and tasty to eat. Many people on a gluten-free diet struggle with eating the same foods and not having enough variety. Learning how to cook gluten-free Indian food will allow you to eat foods prepared in many delicious and healthy ways, and also provide you with extra variety in your meals.

Popular Indian foods today are made with rice, vegetables, lentils, fruits and numerous creative blends of spices. The majority of India's population has embraced vegetarianism, which is widely recognized as being a very healthy diet, however there are still many dishes made with chicken, lamb, seafood and fish. The endless spice blends make Indian food so much fun to eat and to cook, as you can be creative and make foods to suit your personal flavor.

Prepared almost always with fresh ingredients, Indian food is very healthy and good for you to eat. Indian food is not prepared just with

INTRODUCTION

exotic ingredients, but rather with readily available simple whole foods: rice, potatoes, lentils, legumes, vegetables, nuts and dairy products. Foods are sautéed in vegetable oils or ghee and used sparingly.

You do not need expensive or special equipment to make Indian foods, just some good basics: a cutting board, a sharp knife, sauté pans, assorted pots, a roasting pan, a rolling pin. Indian foods are made simply and quickly on the stovetop, which makes cooking perfect for busy modern lifestyles.

Meals in India are usually served all at once, meaning that all 'courses' are laid out on the table at the same time, allowing you to pick and choose what you would like to eat.

Indian food is seasoned with a variety of spices that enhance flavor and give the foods vibrant colors. Traditionally, spices are used whole and are roasted in a hot pan, sometimes dry by themselves and sometimes in oil. The spices are cooked until fragrant and then you continue cooking the recipe. Cooking the spices this way releases the oils and creates a deeper and more intense flavor. When using whole spices they need to be ground, you can grind by hand in a mortar and pestle or use a coffee bean grinder, just make sure to wipe before and after use.

The recipes in this book, list individual spices for most of the recipes, you can substitute with a pre-made blend if it is easier for your lifestyle. If you use store bought blends, roast them in the pan as called for in each recipe, they will taste better. I encourage you to experiment with using the whole spices as the results are much tastier.

The biggest challenge to eating a gluten-free diet is finding tasty and healthy gluten-free bread. The two proteins; gliadian and glutenin, found in wheat (and other gluten containing grains) make good bread products, because they give bread elasticity and structure, making it possible for bread to rise. Grains without these proteins produce denser heavier breads.

Indian breads are most often made in the form of flatbreads and crackers, which are easier to make gluten free. I've included flat bread recipes in this book, made with different types of flours from gluten-free grains, nuts and beans.

- Millet flour is high in B vitamins, fiber, protein and fat. It has a subtle flavor and gives a creamy beige color to your baked goods.
- Almond flour is made from ground up almonds and is high in protein and low in carbohydrates and sugars. The flour gives your baked goods a slightly sweet taste, a soft texture and moisture.
- Chickpea flour made from ground chickpeas is high in protein and carbohydrates; it has a pleasant flavor and a warm golden color.

These flours are healthy options for those eating a gluten free diet. Not only are they gluten free, they are nutritious and they taste good. You can enjoy making the flatbreads in this book knowing they are safe for gluten free diets and healthy for the whole family.

This book brings you the very best of Indian home cooked foods. You will find authentic recipes for every type of Indian dish from gluten-free bread, pickles, chutneys, snacks, desserts, salads, soups, curries and more. I've featured authentic dishes from all of the regions of India. You can take your palate on a tour of India with Shrimp Balcho from the seaside of Goa, to the North India Superstar Butter Chicken, the Ayurvedic Kitchari and savory Punjabi Salad to name a few. The regional cuisines offer subtle differences in techniques, and flavorings, always using local seasonal ingredients.

Enjoy preparing the gluten-free recipes in this book for your family, friends and yourself.

Spices and Ingredients

The ingredients in Indian Cuisine are readily available. I will share with you how I prepare my seasonings and my chicken & vegetable stocks.

Garlic: I use fresh garlic, as the size of garlic cloves can vary, I list a measured amount (1 Tsp, 1 Tbsp) to help you make well seasoned dishes. I purchase fresh garlic, peel it and chop it very finely.

Ginger: I buy fresh ginger root and peel it. I then freeze it in a plastic bag, and grate it fresh for each recipe. Freezing it keeps the flavor and makes grating it much easier.

Cilantro: Is also known as fresh coriander or fresh dhanya.

Ghee: is clarified butter. You can purchase ghee from a supermarket or you can make it at home. Place butter in a small saucepan and melt over medium heat (be careful not to scorch. As the butter warms and melts skim the foamy milk solids off the top. When you have removed the milk solids the butter will be a clear pale yellow liquid. Transfer to a clean glass container and refrigerate, using as needed. If you do not want to use ghee you can use any high quality vegetable oil instead.

Stocks: Many stocks available from the supermarkets contain hidden sources of gluten; however there are easy and affordable alternatives which you can make at home.

In this book the recipes for Lentils, Vegetable and Chicken dishes which use stock as an ingredient, can be made without the stock if required. Simply use the same measurement of water to that of the stock and add ½ tsp of crushed pepper and ½ tsp of garlic.

Basic Chicken Stock

Ingredients:

Left over bones from a roasted chicken.
1 onion, chopped
3 carrots, chopped
2 stalks of celery, chopped
1 tsp garlic, chopped
4 peppercorns
Water (up to 4 liters)

Method:

1. Combine all ingredients in a large pot, add water and bring to a boil.
2. Reduce heat and simmer for 3 hours, skimming off any foam that rises to the top.
3. Allow to cool completely, strain and refrigerate.
4. Use within 1 week or freeze for up to 3 months.

Basic Vegetable Stock

Ingredients:

2 onions, chopped
4 carrots, chopped
10 stalks of celery, chopped
1 tsp garlic, chopped
4 peppercorns
2 bay leaves
1 tbsp vegetable oil

Method:

1. Heat oil in a large pot, add onions, carrots, celery and garlic, cook until vegetables begin to brown.
2. Add water, peppercorns and bay leaves, bring to a boil.
3. Reduce heat and simmer for 2 hours skimming off any foam that rises to the top.
4. Allow to cool completely, strain and refrigerate.
5. Use within 1 week or freeze up to 3 months.

Temperature Guide

This is an **approximate** conversion chart between gas mark and electric ovens.

Gas Mark	Fahrenheit	Celsius	Description
¼	225	110	Very cool/very slow
½	250	130	---
1	275	140	Cool
2	300	150	---
3	325	170	very moderate
4	350	180	moderate
5	375	190	---
6	400	200	moderately hot
7	425	220	hot
8	450	230	---
9	475	240	very hot

This chart should be accurate enough for all your cooking needs, though keep in mind the temperatures will vary between different types, brands, sizes of ovens, fan assisted ovens, in addition to your locations altitude, temperature, humidity, etc.

http://www.onlineconversion.com

Appetizers

Paneer Masala

Prep Time: 15 minutes

Servings: 2

Ingredients:

½ kilo paneer, cut into 1 inch squares
6 tbsp butter
1 tsp oil
2 bay leaves
2 cloves
1 cinnamon stick
2 broken dried red chilies
2 tbsp crushed coriander seeds
1 onion sliced
2 tsp ginger paste
2 tsp garlic paste
1 tsp red chili powder
6 chopped tomatoes
1 tsp salt
120ml water
3 tsp double cream

Method:

1. Heat ½ the butter with oil in a medium sized skillet. Add bay leaves, cloves, cinnamon, red chilies and half of the crushed coriander seeds, sauté for a minute.
2. Add onion and cook for 2 minutes
3. Add ginger paste and garlic paste, cook for another 30 seconds.
4. Add red chili powder and tomatoes. Cook on medium heat till the tomatoes are very soft, puree the mixture.

5. Put the puree back in the pan, adding the remaining butter, cook until the butter melts.
6. Add paneer, salt and the water.
7. Cook covered on low heat for five minutes.
8. Remove from heat and stir in cream.
9. Serve immediately, garnished with remaining crushed coriander seeds.

Chick Pea Fritters

Prep Time: 30 minutes

Servings: 4

Ingredients:

1 can of rinsed and drained chickpeas
½ cup sliced scallions
½ cup chopped cilantro
½ cup chickpea flour
1 large egg
1 tsp coarse salt
Vegetable oil

Method:

1. Place chickpeas, scallions, and cilantro in food processor and pulse until a coarse paste forms. Pulse in flour, egg, and salt.
2. Use ¼ Cup of mixture to form patties. These are round in shape and slightly flattened.
3. Heat 1/4 inch vegetable oil in a large skillet over medium high heat.
4. Once the oil is heated add chickpea patties.
5. Cook patties for 4-5 minutes until golden brown on both sides.

Note: this dish can be made without egg. Simply use a tbsp of arrowroot powder as an alternative.

APPETIZERS

Vegetable Pakora

Prep Time: 30 minutes

Servings: 4

Ingredients:

1 cup chickpea flour
½ tsp ground coriander
1 tsp salt
½ tsp ground turmeric
½ tsp chili powder
½ tsp garam masala
2 cloves garlic, crushed
325ml water
Vegetable oil for deep frying
½ head cauliflower florets, cut into mini florets
2 onions sliced thinly

Method:

1. Sift the chickpea flour into a medium bowl.
2. Mix in the coriander, salt, turmeric, chili powder, garam masala and garlic.
3. Add the water to the dry ingredients and mix to form a thick, smooth batter.
4. Heat vegetable oil over medium high heat in a large, heavy saucepan, heat the oil to 190 °C/ 375° F.
5. Dip the cauliflower florets and onions in the batter and fry them in small batches until golden brown, about 4 to 5 minutes.

Papri Chat

Prep Time: 40 minutes

Servings: 4

Papri

Ingredients:

1 cup millet flour
1 tbsp ghee
Salt
Water
Vegetable oil for deep frying

Chat

Ingredients:

2 boil potatoes diced into small cubes
1 tin of chickpeas (microwave for 5 mins)
1 onion finely chopped
Yoghurt
Coriander leaves
Chutney of your choice

Method:

1. In a bowl add the millet flour, oil, and salt and combine.
2. Slowly add water and make a smooth dough. Leave aside covered with damp cloth for 15 minutes.
3. Knead the dough again for a few minutes until it is smooth and elastic.
4. Pinch off some dough and make small balls. Roll out small thin

APPETIZERS

rotis, about 4 cm in diameter. Use a fork to make indents into each roti.
5. Heat vegetable oil over medium high heat in a large, heavy saucepan, heat the oil to 190 °C/ 375° F.
6. Place the roti into the hot oil and cook for at least 2 minutes on each side. Flip over and fry the other side till light golden brown and fairly hard. Allow roti to cool before applying the Chat.
7. Layer the mini rotis in a serving dish, with boiled potato and chickpeas.
8. Garnish with your favorite chutneys, yoghurt, sprinkle some chopped onion and coriander leaves.
9. Serve immediately.

Chicken Pakora

Prep Time: 30 minutes

Servings: 2

Ingredients:

1/3 kilo of diced chicken
1 tbsp vegetable oil
2 bay leaves
2 cloves
1 cinnamon stick
2 broken dried red chilies
1 tbsp crushed coriander seeds
220g chickpea flour
1 tsp salt
¼ tsp chili powder
½ tsp turmeric powder
Millet flour to coat the chicken
Water
Vegetable oil for deep-frying

Method:

1. Heat oil in a medium sized skillet.
2. Add bay leaves, cloves, cinnamon, red chilies and half of the crushed coriander seeds. Sauté for one minute.
3. Add the diced chicken and mix well, fry for 10 minutes on a moderate heat.
4. Remove the chicken (separating the cloves, cinnamon, chilies and bay leaves),
5. Drain the chicken on kitchen paper and allow to cool completely.
6. In a large bowl mix together the chickpea flour, salt, chili powder

APPETIZERS

and turmeric. Add enough water to form a thick batter.

7. Heat vegetable oil over medium high heat in a large, heavy saucepan, heat the oil to 190 °C/ 375° F.
8. Coat the cooked chicken with a little Millet flour then dip into the batter and deep fry until golden brown.
9. Drain and serve hot with a chutney of your choice.

Potato & Spinach Pies

Prep Time: 50 minutes

Servings: 4

Ingredients:

½ kilo potatoes, peeled and cubed
4 tbsp butter
1 onion, chopped
1 tbsp cumin seeds
1 tbsp poppy seeds
1 tbsp black mustard seeds
2 tbsp finely chopped ginger
2 red chilies, halved, deseeded and sliced
3 tbsp red curry paste
340g spinach, chopped
4 tomatoes, chopped
4 eggs, beaten
3 tbsp cilantro chopped

Method:

1. Heat oven to 190 °C/ 375° F.
2. To make the filling, heat a pan of salted water. When boiling, add potatoes and boil for 15 minutes until tender.
3. Melt the butter in a pan and sauté the onions until tender, add cumin, mustard seeds, ginger and chilies, stirring occasionally, for about 6 minutes until soft.
4. Stir in curry paste, spinach and tomatoes.
5. When the spinach and tomatoes are cooked add the cubed potatoes, stirring vigorously to break them apart a bit, add salt and the fresh cilantro.

APPETIZERS

6. Add eggs and mix well.
7. Fill muffin cup ¾'s full of mixture, then top with the remaining butter and sprinkle with poppy seeds.
8. Bake for 25 minutes until bubbling and crisp on top.

Lamb Meatballs

Prep Time: 25 minutes

Servings: 4

Ingredients:

½ kilo ground lamb
120g finely chopped white onion
1 tbsp chopped fresh mint
1 tbsp chopped fresh cilantro
1 garlic clove, chopped
1 tsp ground coriander
1 tsp salt
½ tsp ground cumin
¼ tsp cinnamon
¼ tsp freshly ground black pepper

Method:

1. Heat the oven to 190 °C/ 375° F.
2. Combine all ingredients in a large bowl and mix thoroughly.
3. Form into 30 balls and place on a baking sheet.
4. Bake until meatballs are no longer pink in the middle, about 15 minutes.

APPETIZERS

Potato Fritters

Prep Time: 20 minutes (plus 15 mins to boil potatoes)

Servings: 4

Ingredients:

200g mashed sweet potato
200g ricotta
120g icing sugar plus more for dusting
1 tsp cinnamon
Salt
120g millet flour
½ tsp baking powder
½ tsp baking soda
Vegetable oil for frying

Method:

1. Heat vegetable oil over medium high heat in a large, heavy saucepan. Heat the oil to 190 °C/ 375° F.
2. In a large bowl combine the potato, ricotta, sugar, cinnamon and salt until smooth.
3. Sift together the millet flour, baking powder and baking soda and add to the potato mixture. Mix all ingredients together.
4. Drop heaped teaspoons of the batter into the hot oil, work in batches to avoid overcrowding the pot. Turn as needed, fry until golden brown. Drain on paper towels.
5. Dust with confectioners' sugar and a pinch of salt.

Onion Fritters

Prep Time: 20 minutes

Servings: 4

Ingredients:

325g chickpea flour
1 tbsp crushed red pepper
1 tsp salt
½ tsp baking powder
1 green chili pepper, sliced
3 tbsp cilantro leaves,
1 onion, chopped
225ml water

Method:

1. Heat vegetable oil over medium high heat in a large, heavy saucepan. Heat the oil to 190 °C/ 375° F.
2. In a large bowl, mix together the chickpea flour, crushed red pepper, salt, baking powder, sliced chili pepper, cilantro.
3. Add the water and mix vigorously until the batter is thick and smooth, then add the sliced onions.
4. Once the oil is heated, add heaping teaspoons of batter into the hot oil.
5. Work in batches to avoid overcrowding the pan.
6. Fry the pakoras until they are a dark golden brown.
7. Drain on paper towels and keep in a hot oven until all the fritters are fried.
8. Serve immediately.

APPETIZERS

Cassava Chips

Prep Time: 20 minutes (plus 20 mins boiling cassava)

Servings: 4

Ingredients:

1 kilo cassava
Salt
Vegetable oil for frying.

Method:

1. Peel and slice the cassava and boil in salted water till al dente. 2. Drain and keep aside.
3. Heat vegetable oil over medium high heat in a large, heavy saucepan, heat the oil to 190 °C/ 375° F.
4. In small batches fry the cassava chips until light golden brown.
5. Drain on kitchen paper.
6. Keep warm in a hot oven until all chips are cooked.
7. Serve immediately.

Fish Pakoras

Prep Time: 20 minutes

Servings: 4

Ingredients:

4 white fish fillets, cooked and chopped into bite size pieces
2 eggs
½ tsp salt
½ tsp red chili powder
2 tbsp corn meal
2 tbsp lemon juice
1 tsp chopped coriander leaves
Vegetable oil for deep frying

Method

1. Heat vegetable oil over medium high heat in a large, heavy saucepan, heat the oil to 190 °C/ 375° F.
2. Mix the eggs, salt, chili powder, corn meal, lemon juice and coriander leaves together to make a batter.
3. Dip fish pieces into the batter and fry in batches till golden and crisp all over.

APPETIZERS

Kachoris

Prep Time: 50 minutes

Servings: 4

Filling

Ingredients:

200g yellow lentils
200g cooked, mashed potato
1 tbsp butter
1 tsp salt
½ tsp cinnamon, ground
¼ tsp cardamom, ground
¼ tsp black pepper
¼ tsp garlic powder
¼ tsp onion powder
1/8 tsp ground ginger
¼ tsp ground cumin
½ tsp paprika

Dough

Ingredients:

200g millet flour
200g chickpea flour
1 tsp salt
2 tsp oil
350ml hot water
Vegetable oil for deep frying

Method:

1. In a processor, blend the cooked lentils and potatoes until a paste forms.
2. Add the butter, salt and spices, and blend until smooth.
3. Heat a non-stick pan over medium high heat
4. Put the potato-lentil mixture into it. Stirring vigorously.
5. Cook the potato lentil mixture until it forms a ball and pulls away from the pan – this should take 5-6 minutes.
6. Set aside.
7. In a bowl, combine millet flour, chickpea flour, and salt. Stir in the oil and mix until the oil is evenly distributed. Add the water 120ml at a time and knead together until a sticky dough forms. Let the dough rest for 10 minutes.
8. Divide the dough into 12 equal portions. Flatten each dough ball into a 4 inch disk. Fill each disk with the cooked potato-lentil paste. Form a ball around the paste, bringing the edges of the dough together and pinching to seal. Flatten the balls slightly.
9. Heat enough oil to come halfway up the kachoris, to 190 °C/ 375° F in a skillet.
10. Place a few kachoris at a time in the oil, and fry until golden brown. Drain on paper towels. Serve immediately.

APPETIZERS

Chicken Kofta

Prep Time: 60 minutes

Servings: 4

Ingredients:

½ kilo chicken, ground
1 onion, chopped
3 cloves roasted garlic, chopped
1 tsp white pepper
1 tsp cumin
2 tbsp cilantro, chopped
1 tbsp mint leaves chopped
½ tsp chili flakes
½ tsp salt
Pinch of cloves

Method:

1. Mix the ground chicken and all the ingredients in a large bowl.
2. Mix for at least 5 minutes until everything is combined.
3. Let the kofta mixture rest for 20 to 30 minutes in a cool place to marinate.
4. Wet your hands with cold water. Divide the kofta into 6 equal portions and roll each portion into a log.
5. Put a long skewer up through the center.
6. Repeat skewering until done.
7. Cook over a charcoal grill.
8. Serve hot.

Onion & Rice Bhajis

Prep Time: 30 minutes

Servings: 4

Ingredients:

½ kilo left over rice
120g chickpea flour
1 onion chopped
3 to 4 green chilies chopped
1 tbsp grated ginger
1 tbsp garlic, chopped
3 tbsp cilantro leaves, chopped
3 tbsp mint leaves, chopped
Salt
Vegetable oil for deep-frying

Method:

1. Mash the rice and add the onion, ginger, garlic, chilies, coriander leaves and mint leaves and mix well.
2. Add the chickpea flour and salt little by little to the rice mixture, just enough to bind the mixture, do not add more than needed
3. Heat vegetable oil over medium high heat in a large, heavy saucepan, heat the oil to 190 °C/ 375°F.
4. Form a round patty with 1 tablespoon of mixture and fry patties until golden brown on all the sides.
5. Remove and drain on paper towels.
6. Serve it immediately.

APPETIZERS

Carrot Dosai

Prep Time: 60 minutes (plus 20 hrs dhal soaking time)

Servings: 4

Ingredients:

Dosa

300g rice
200g urad dal

Carrot Filling

3 carrots, grated
2 onions, chopped
1 tbsp yellow curry powder
3-4 green chilies, chopped
2 tbsp oil
¼ tsp black mustard seeds
Salt

Method:

Dosa Batter :

1. Mix the rice and urad dal, wash them with water 4-5 times. Then soak them in water for 6-8 hours.
2. Drain water, add salt and grind the mixture in blender or food processor to make a smooth batter.
3. Cover it and keep it at room temperature, allow it to ferment for 12 hours.
4. After fermentation the batter will rise and become very creamy and bubbly, this is how you know it has fermented properly.

Carrot Filling :

Method:

1. Peel and grate carrots.
2. Heat oil in a pan, add mustard seeds, onion, curry powder and green chili. Fry on medium heat for 2 minutes.
3. Add grated carrots to the pan and cook for 5 minutes.

Carrot Dosa :

Method:

1. Heat a non-stick flat pan over medium-high flame.
2. Spray pan liberally with pan spray.
3. Pour 1/2 cup of dosa batter and spread it properly in a circular motion to form a circle. (Similar to how you make pancakes).
4. Allow to cook until the outer edges are done.
5. Add 1/2 tablespoon of oil to the dosa crust.
6. After 2 minutes or so, you will find brown spots on the dosa. Immediately spread 2 tablespoons of carrot filling on the surface of dosa and flip the 2 sides of the dosa one over the other, such that the carrot filling is covered.
7. Crispy carrot dosa is ready to serve.

Chutneys/Sauces

Raita

Prep Time: 10 minutes

Servings: 4

Ingredients:

475ml plain yogurt
2 fresh scallions, sliced
1-2 fresh green chilies, finely chopped
1 tbsp ginger root, grated
1 garlic clove, finely chopped
1 cucumber, chopped into small cubes
1 tsp cumin seeds, toasted
Juice of 1 lemon
1 tsp salt
½ tsp cracked black pepper corns

Method:

1. Combine and stir all ingredients.
2. Chill until ready to serve.

CHUTNEYS/SAUCES

Roasted Garlic Raita

Prep Time: 10 minutes

Servings: 4

Ingredients:

1 head garlic, roasted and chopped
4 tbsp olive oil
475ml plain yogurt
1 cayenne pepper, diced
2 tbsp finely chopped onion
¾ tsp salt
¾ tsp pepper
3 tbsp fresh mint, chopped

Method:

1. Combine and stir all ingredients.
2. Chill until ready to serve.

Mint Sauce

Prep Time: 10 minutes

Servings: 4

Ingredients:

1 bunch cilantro leaves
½ cup mint leaves
1½ green chilies (small, start with one & increase heat if needed)
1 lime
Salt

Method:

1. Combine all ingredients in a blender or food processor, blend until smooth, add salt and chilies to taste.
2. Chill until ready to serve.

CHUTNEYS/SAUCES

Tomato & Ginger Chutney

Prep Time: 40 minutes

Servings: 4

Ingredients:

2 tbsp vegetable oil
1 medium onion, chopped
2 tsp garlic, chopped
1 tbsp ginger, grated
2 pounds fresh chopped plum tomatoes
120ml red-wine vinegar
90g packed light-brown sugar
75g raisins

Method:

1. In a saucepan, heat oil over medium heat. Add onion, garlic, and ginger.
2. Cook, stirring, until onion is softened.
3. Add tomatoes, vinegar, brown sugar, and raisins.
4. Simmer, until thick and jam-like, 25 to 30 minutes.
5. Cool completely.
6. Chill until ready to serve.

Apple Chutney

Prep Time: 40 minutes

Servings: 4

Ingredients:

2 large apples, peeled, cored, and chopped
75g onion, chopped
60ml red wine vinegar
45g brown sugar
1 tbsp orange zest
1 tbsp ginger, grated
½ tsp allspice

Method:

1. Combine all ingredients in a medium saucepan and stir well. Bring to a boil; reduce heat and simmer, for 30 minutes.
2. Cool completely.
3. Chill until ready to serve.

CHUTNEYS/SAUCES

Coriander Chutney

Prep Time: 15 minutes

Servings: 4

Ingredients:

1 bunch coriander leaves
3 green chilies
1 bunch green scallions
3 tbsp coconut, grated
1 tsp tamarind paste
Salt
2 tsp oil

For the seasoning:

Ingredients:

1 tsp oil
1 tsp mustard seeds

Method:

1. Heat 2 tsps of oil in a pan, add scallions, green chilies and saute until onions are translucent.
2. Add coriander, grated coconut, tamarind and turn off the heat, allow coriander leaves to wilt.
3. Once mixture is cool, blend in a blender or food processor with salt and a little water into a smooth paste.
4. Heat1 tsp of oil in a pan, toast mustard seeds until fragrant.
5. Add to chutney and mix well.
6. Cool completely. Chill until ready to serve.

Tamarind Chutney

Prep Time: 40 minutes

Servings: 4

Ingredients:

1 tbsp vegetable oil
1 tsp cumin seeds
1 tsp ground ginger
½ tsp cayenne pepper
½ tsp fennel seeds
½ tsp asafoetida powder
½ tsp garam masala
475ml water
225g white sugar
3 tbsp tamarind paste

Method:

1. Heat the oil in a saucepan over medium heat. Add the cumin seeds, ginger, cayenne pepper, fennel seeds, asafoetida powder, and garam masala; cook until fragrant.
2. Add the water to the pan with the spices, sugar and tamarind paste.
3. Bring to a boil, then simmer over low heat until the mixture turns a deep brown and is thick enough to coat the back of a metal spoon. This should take 20 to 30 minutes.
4. Cool completely. Chill until ready to serve.

CHUTNEYS/SAUCES

Coconut Chutney

Prep Time: 10 minutes

Servings: 4

Ingredients:

½ fresh coconut, grated
1 tsp mustard seeds
1 tsp yellow curry powder
2 dry red chilies
Salt to taste
2 tbsp oil

Method:

1. Grind the coconut into a fine paste in the food processor.
2. In a small pan, heat the oil.
3. Once the oil is hot add the mustard seeds, curry powder, dry red chilies.
4. Fry till the red chilies turn dark in color.
5. Remove from the fire and add to the coconut paste.
6. Add salt to taste and serve.

Red Chili Chutney

Prep Time: 20 minutes

Servings: 4

Ingredients:

8-10 fresh red chilies
8 ripe red peppers
Olive oil
2 medium red onions, chopped
1 sprig fresh rosemary, chopped
2 bay leaves
1 stick cinnamon
Salt
Black pepper
90g brown sugar
180ml balsamic vinegar

Method:

1. Roast chilies and peppers in an oven, until browned.
2. Allow peppers and chilies to cool, then remove the skin and seeds and chop in a food processor.
3. Heat oil saucepan, add onions, rosemary, bay leaves and cinnamon, season with a little salt and pepper, cook until the onions are soft and very golden.
4. Add the chopped peppers, chilies, sugar and the vinegar to the onions and keep cooking.
5. When the liquid reduces season to taste.
6. Take out the cinnamon stick and the bay leaves.
7. Cool completely. Chill until ready to serve.

CHUTNEYS/SAUCES

Curried Onion Chutney

Prep Time: 10 minutes

Servings: 4

Ingredients:

110g finely chopped onion
1 tbsp tomatoe ketchup
¾ tsp curry powder
½ tsp ground mustard
2 tsp sugar
1 tbsp white vinegar

Method:

1. Stir all ingredients into a small bowl until combined.
2. Serve immediately or cover and chill until ready to serve.

Mango Pickle

Prep Time: 20 minutes

Servings: 4

Ingredients:

1 kilo raw green mangoes (cut into 8 pieces each)
200g salt
3 tbsp aniseed/fennel
1½ tbsp mustard seeds
3 tbsp onion seeds
1 tbsp fenugreek seeds
5 tbsp red chili powder
2 tsp turmeric powder
700ml mustard oil

Method:

1. Sterilize and dry a glass jar.
2. Put the mangoes in the jar and cover with salt. Mix well and cover the jar tightly.
3. Leave the jar out in the sun for a week so that the mangoes soften.
4. Mix the aniseed/fennel, mustard, onion and fenugreek seeds, chili powder and turmeric together.
5. Add this spice mix to the mangoes.
6. Heat the mustard oil till it smokes and then turn off the heat. Allow the oil to cool fully.
7. Pour this oil over the mangoes so that all the pieces are submerged. Mix well.
8. Put the tightly covered jar back in the sunlight for two weeks. Mix well every few days for the next two weeks.
9. Once the mangos have fermented well, store the jar in a cool place. Normally mango pickles made in this way will last up to six months.

Carrot Pickle

Prep Time: 20 minutes

Servings: 4

Ingredients:

½ kilo carrots, peeled and cut into ½ inch cubes
6 tbsp vegetable oil
1 tsp turmeric powder
2 tsp fennel seeds
1 tsp mustard seeds
½ tsp fenugreek seeds
1 tsp salt
1 tbsp ginger minced
Juice of 1 lime/lemon

Method:

1. Heat the oil in a deep pan, on medium heat, till very hot. Add the whole spices and fry until fragrant.
2. Add the carrots, salt and ginger. Mix well. Stir often and cook till carrots are slightly soft. Remove from heat.
3. When cooled slightly, add the lime/lemon juice.
4. Put the pickle into a sterilized jar with a tight lid.
5. Keep in the sun daily for 2 weeks. This will cause the pickle flavors to develop nicely.

Salads/ Soups

Sweet Potato Soup

Prep Time: 50 minutes

Servings: 4

Ingredients:

3 sweet potatoes, peeled and sliced into 1 inch rounds
4 tbsp of olive oil
1 onion, chopped
2 garlic cloves, finely chopped
2 stalks of celery, chopped
1 tbsp of garam masala
1 tsp of curry powder
1 tsp sea salt
950ml of vegetable stock
240ml of coconut milk
120ml of water

Method:

1. Pre-heat the oven to 190 °C/ 375°F.
2. Season potatoes with salt and place on a roasting pan, drizzle with 2 tbsp of olive oil.
3. Roast for 30 minutes or until tender.
4. Remove from oven and set aside to cool.
5. While potatoes are roasting, heat the remaining olive oil over medium heat, in a large soup pot.
6. Add the onion and celery cook until onions and celery are soft. Add garlic and cook for 2 minutes.
7. Add garam masala and curry powder. Cook stirring constantly for 30 seconds.
8. Once potatoes are cooked in the oven, add the potatoes to the pot

SALADS/ SOUPS

and stir well to combine.
9. Add stock and bring to the boil. Reduce heat to low and simmer soup for 15 minutes.
10. Remove soup from heat and cool. Ladle soup into a blender or food processor and blend in batches until smooth and creamy. Add coconut milk stir well to combine. Serve immediately.

Carrot & Beetroot Soup

Prep Time: 40 minutes

Servings: 4

Ingredients:

3 beets washed, peeled and chopped
4 carrots, peeled and chopped
2 tsp garlic, chopped
1 tbsp ginger, grated
2 onions, chopped
1 green chili, seeded and chopped
¼ tsp cinnamon
½ tsp cumin
½ tsp red chili flakes
2 tbsp oil
Salt
Fresh cracked black pepper
1.5 liters water

Method:

1. Heat oil in a large soup pot, add onions and chilies and cook until tender.
2. Add garlic, ginger, cinnamon, cumin & red chili flakes stirring well.
3. Add beetroot and carrots and water. Bring to a boil, reduce heat and simmer for 30 minutes or until beetroot and carrot are tender.
4. Puree in blender or food processor until smooth, add salt and pepper to taste.

SALADS/ SOUPS

Sweet Corn and Chicken Soup

Prep Time: 50 minutes

Servings: 4

Ingredients:

4 tbsp ghee
¾ kilo diced boneless, skinless chicken thighs
300g corn kernels
2 tbsp garam masala
1 onion chopped
75g carrots, chopped
75g celery, chopped
1 tbsp garlic, chopped
2 tbsp ginger, grated
300g Granny Smith apples peeled, cored and diced
1.5liters chicken stock
¾ tsp freshly ground black pepper
350ml unsweetened coconut milk
285g basmati rice
3 tbsp chopped fresh cilantro leaves

Method:

1. Heat ghee in a soup pot over medium heat, add chicken and garam masala.
2. Cook until chicken begins to turn golden brown, add the onions, carrots and celery and corn to the hot pan and cook until lightly caramelized, about 4 to 5 minutes.
3. Add the garlic, ginger and apples to the pan and saute until the apples are caramelized, about 7 to 8 minutes.
4. Add the chicken stock, rice and coconut milk, add salt and pepper

to taste, simmer soup for 30 minutes on low heat.
5. Serve immediately. Garnish with cilantro.

SALADS/ SOUPS

Tomato Soup

Prep Time: 30 minutes

Servings: 4

Soup

Ingredients:

600g plum or vine tomatoes, chopped
2 carrots peeled and chopped
2 celery sticks, chopped
2 tbsp ginger, grated
2 tbsp oil
½ tsp salt, adjust to taste
½ tsp sugar, adjust to taste
1/8 tsp black pepper
350ml vegetable stock

Seasoning:

Ingredients:

1tsp oil
½ tsp cumin seed
Pinch of asafetida
1tbsp cilantro

Method:

1. Heat the oil in soup pot over medium heat add ginger, carrot and celery cook until tender.
2. Add the tomatoes, salt, sugar and pepper let it cook until tomatoes are soft.

3. Puree soup in blender or food processor.
4. For seasoning; heat the oil in a soup pot add the cumin seed and asafetida. As cumin seeds crack add cilantro and stir for a minute then add the tomato mixture and stock.
5. Let soup simmer over low heat for 10 minutes. Serve immediately.

SALADS/ SOUPS

Spinach Soup

Prep Time: 25 minutes

Servings: 4

Ingredients:

3 big bunches spinach, thoroughly washed, dried and chopped
1 cinnamon stick
3 cloves
1 bay leaf
1 onion, chopped
3 garlic cloves, chopped
1 tbsp ginger grated
1 green chili
1 tbsp ghee
700ml vegetable stock
2 tbsp rice flour mixed in 2 tbsp water
Fresh cracked black pepper
Salt

Method:

1. Heat the ghee in a soup pot over medium heat, add garlic, cloves, cinnamon, bay leaf, and cook until seasonings are fragrant. Add the onions, garlic and ginger, cook for 5 minutes.
2. Add the chopped spinach, green chili and cook for 2 minutes. Add vegetable stock, and simmer for 6-8 minutes.
3. Discard the cloves, bay leaf and cinnamon stick.
4. Puree the spinach-onion mixture, return to the heat, add salt and black pepper and simmer for 6-8 minutes.
5. Add the rice flour mixture and stir until the soup thickens.
6. Serve immediately.

Pepper Rasam

Prep Time: 40 minutes

Servings: 4

Rasam

Ingredients:

95g tamarind
4 cloves of garlic chopped
1 generous pinch of asafetida
¼ tsp turmeric powder
1 tomato, chopped
4 cup of water
Salt to taste

Pepper Rasam seasoning

Ingredients:

To dry roast (roast without oil)
2-4 dry red chilis
2 tbsp of channa dal
1 tbsp of toor dhal
2 tbsp of coriander seeds
1 tbsp of black peppercorns
½ tbsp. cumin seeds
6 curry leaves

Final Seasoning:

Ingredients:

1 tbsp of ghee

SALADS/ SOUPS

¼ tsp of mustard seeds
¼ tsp Cumin Seed

Method:

1. Dry roast chilies, spices and dals, until the dals turn golden brown. (Pepper Rasam seasoning ingredients). Keep the heat low and mix constantly to ensure uniform browning. Cool completely, grind to a powder, and set aside.
2. Soak the tamarind in a cup of warm water, extract juice and discard pulp.
3. In a soup pot over medium heat add the tamarind, garlic, asafoetida, turmeric, chopped tomato, salt. Bring to a boil, and simmer for 5 minutes before adding spice mixture.
4. Continue to simmer for 20-25 minutes, until the tamarind flavor mellows.
5. Heat the ghee in a small pan. Add final seasoning ingredients, mustard and cumin seeds when they become fragrant add to the rasam. Adjust salt.
6. Serve immediately.

Bean Salad

Prep Time: 10 minutes

Servings: 2

Ingredients:

300g chickpeas
6 roma tomatoes, chopped
2 carrots, shredded
1 cucumber, halved lengthwise, seeded and thinly sliced
½ cup red onion, thinly sliced
1 tbsp lemon zest
Juice of 1 lemon
3 tbsp olive oil
1 tsp ground cumin
1 tsp curry powder
½ tsp salt
¼ tsp ground black pepper

Method:

1. In a large bowl combine all ingredients, mix well to combine and distribute flavors.
2. Chill before serving.

SALADS/ SOUPS

Vegetable Salad

Prep Time: 10 minutes

Servings: 2

Ingredients:

4 large lettuce leaves
1 sweet onion, chopped
2 tomatoes, chopped
2 cucumbers, chopped
3 tbsp mint leaves, chopped
3 tbsp cilantro, chopped
Juice of ½ lemon
Lemon slices for garnish
½ tsp cumin powder
¼ tsp red chili powder
Fresh cracked black pepper
Salt

Method:

1. Place lettuce leaves on a medium sized salad plate.
2. In a bowl combine all other ingredients, mix well to combine and distribute flavors.

Punjabi Salad

Prep Time: 10 minutes

Servings: 2

Salad

Ingredients:

75g carrots, chopped small
75g cabbage, chopped small
75g capsicum, chopped small
75g onion, chopped small
75g tomato, seeded and chopped small
300g paneer, chopped and fried in oil

Dressing

Ingredients:

1 tsp fresh cracked black pepper
1 tsp ground cumin
2 tbsp olive oil
Salt
Juice of ¼ lemon
Green onions
Cilantro

Method:

1. Mix all the ingredients of dressing in a small bowl.
2. Toss dressing with vegetables.
3. Chill before serving.
4. Garnish with green onions and cilantro.

SALADS/ SOUPS

Onion/Tomato Salad

Prep Time: 10 minutes

Servings: 2

Ingredients:

6 Roma tomatoes seeded and chopped
150g onion, chopped
1 tsp toasted crushed cumin seed
½ tsp red chili flakes
Juice of 1 lemon
3 tbsp cilantro
3 tbsp mint
Fresh cracked black pepper
Salt

Method:

1. Combine all ingredients in a bowl, toss well to combine and distribute flavors, add salt and pepper to taste.
2. Chill Before serving.

Vegetable and Lentil Curries

Red Chori Lentil Curry

Prep Time: 60 minutes (plus 8 hrs soaking time for beans)

Servings: 4

Ingredients:

½ kilo red chori (adzuki) beans soaked water for 6 to 8 hours
1 liter water
1 onion chopped
2 tomatoes chopped
2 tbsp ghee
2 tbsp ginger grated
1 tbsp garlic, chopped
4 green chilies
¼ tsp turmeric powder
2 tsp garam masala
Salt
60ml yogurt
3 tbsp cilantro
¼ tsp of black mustard seeds
8 curry leaves

Method:

1. Drain and rinse red chori beans, cook on stovetop in water with ½ tsp salt, over medium heat until beans are tender.
2. In a large pan heat ghee over medium heat, add mustard seeds and curry leaves. Once the mustard seeds start to pop add onions, cook until tender.
3. Add garlic, chilies, ginger and tomatoes. Cook until tomatoes are very soft.
4. Add red chori beans, turmeric and garam masala, simmer for 30

VEGETABLE AND LENTIL CURRIES

minutes over low heat.
5. Garnish with yogurt and cilantro. Serve immediately.

Yellow Curry with Cauliflower and Squash

Prep Time: 30 minutes

Servings: 4

Ingredients:

1 cauliflower, cut into small pieces
1 onion, chopped
2 squash chopped
3 carrots, peeled and sliced
2 garlic cloves, chopped
2 tbsp olive oil
350ml water
1 can of coconut milk
2 tbsp red curry paste
2 tsp dried basil
1½ tsp curry powder
1 tsp coriander powder
Salt
½ tsp cumin seeds

Method:

1. In a large pan over medium heat add olive oil and cumin seeds. Allow the seeds to ferment then add onions, squash, garlic, cauliflower and carrots, basil, coriander and curry powders and salt to taste into the pot and cook for 7-8 minutes.
2. Add the water, curry paste and the coconut milk, simmer for 15-20 minutes or until vegetables are soft.

Green Curry with Sweet Potatoes and Peppers

Prep Time: 20 minutes

Servings: 4

Ingredients:

2 red bell peppers, cut into ½ inch strips
1 onion, thinly sliced
2 medium sweet potatoes, peeled and cut into ½ moons
1 tbsp oil
1 tbsp garlic, chopped
2 tbsp green curry paste
350ml coconut milk
120ml water
1 tbsp cilantro, chopped
Salt
Fresh cracked black pepper

Method:

1. In a large pan over medium high heat oil and sauté peppers, onions and sweet potatoes until they begin to get golden, about 5 minutes. Add garlic and curry paste stir well and cook for 1 minute.
2. Add coconut milk and water, then simmer until potatoes are tender, about 10 minutes.
3. Stir in cilantro and adjust salt and pepper to taste

Kitchari

Prep Time: 60 minutes (plus soaking time 3 hrs)

Servings: 4

Ingredients:

190g split or whole mung dal
190g Basmati rice
1 tbsp ginger, grated
1 tbsp unsweetened coconut, shredded
3 tbsp cilantro, chopped
120ml water
3 tbsp ghee
1 cinnamon stick
5 whole cardamom pods
5 whole cloves
10 black peppercorns
3 bay leaves
½ tsp turmeric
Salt
1.5- 2 liters water

Method:

1. Soak the split mung dal for 3-5 hours in hot water.
2. Rinse the mung dal and rice until the water is clear.
3. In a blender or food processor, combine ginger, coconut, cilantro and 120ml of water. Blend until smooth.
4. In a large saucepan over medium heat, add ghee, cinnamon, cloves, cardamom pods, peppercorn and bay leaves. Cook until fragrant
5. Add the blended items to the spices, and then the turmeric, stir for a moment until lightly browned.

VEGETABLE AND LENTIL CURRIES

6. Stir in mung dal and rice and mix well
7. Pour in 1.5liters of water, cover and bring to a boil. Let it boil for 5-10 minutes, then turn down the heat to low and cook, lightly covered.
8. Cook until dal and rice are soft, about 35-45 min. Add more water if needed. Adjust salt and pepper to taste.

Roasted Root Vegetable Curry

Prep Time: 40 minutes

Servings: 4

Ingredients:

5 carrots, peeled and cut into 1-inch pieces
3 parsnips, peeled and cut into 1-inch pieces
2 turnips, peeled and cut into 1-inch pieces
1 red onion, cut into 1-inch chunks
8 large garlic cloves
2 tsp madras curry powder
60ml vegetable oil
Salt
Freshly ground black pepper
3 tbsp cilantro, chopped

Method:

1. Preheat oven to 190 °C/ 375°F.
2. In a small pan over medium heat, toast the curry powder, shaking the pan occasionally, until fragrant, about 1 minute, remove the pan from the heat.
3. Mix oil, salt and pepper with the curry powder. Put the carrots, parsnips, turnip, onion and garlic in a big bowl and toss well with seasoned oil to cover vegetables.
4. Place vegetables in a single layer on a large roasting pan and roast the vegetables until they are tender, about 30 minutes.
5. Garnish with cilantro and serve immediately.

Plaintain Tomato Kofta

Prep Time: 60 minutes

Servings: 4

Kofta Balls

Ingredients:

4 plantains cut into 1 inch pieces
2 green chilies
1 tbsp ginger, grated
3 tbsp cilantro
40g cashews
Salt

For Paste

Ingredients:

150g onion, finely chopped
3 chopped tomatoes
2 green chilies
1 tbsp ginger, grated,
1 tbsp garlic, chopped
1 tbsp cumin seeds
½ tsp turmeric
½ tbsp chili powder
1 tbsp ghee
Vegetable oil

Method:

1. Cook plantains in water until soft.

2. Drain and mash plantains. Add ¼ cup finely chopped cashew nuts, 1 tbsp ginger, 2 green chopped chilies, salt and chopped cilantro.
3. Roll mixture into small balls and deep fry in oil.
4. In a sauté pan over medium heat add 1tbsp ghee and 2tbsp oil, add onions, and tomatoes, cook until soft.
5. Blend the tomato based gravy and return to sauté pan.
6. In a food processor make the paste. Blend the ginger, garlic, green chili, cumin seeds and cashews into a smooth paste, add water as needed.
7. Return the paste to the pan and add the turmeric, chili powder and salt, reduce heat and let simmer for about 8-10 minutes.
8. Add the fried plantain balls and cook for 2-3 more minutes.
9. Garnish with fresh cilantro. Serve immediately.

Paneer & Green Pea Curry

Prep Time: 20 minutes

Servings: 4

Ingredients:

½ kilo paneer cubed
150g green peas
1 onion, ground
3 tomatoes, ground
1 tbsp ginger, grated
2 tbsp garlic chopped
2 tsp coriander powder
1 tsp cumin powder
2 tsp garam masala
½ tsp of cumin seeds
½ tsp turmeric powder
2 green chilies chopped fine
6 tbsp of oil
350ml water
Salt
3 tbsp heavy cream
Fresh cilantro & mint leaves for garnish

Method:

1. Grind onions and tomatoes into a fine paste in a food processor or blender. Keep aside.
2. In a medium sized pan over medium high heat add 2-3tbsp of oil in a pan and saute the cubes of paneer until golden. Drain onto a paper towel.
3. In the same pan heat 2-3 tbsp of oil, add cumin seeds. Once seeds

had browned, add the onion & tomato paste. Fry till it turns light brown, add ginger and garlic and cook for 2 minutes.
4. Add the coriander, cumin, turmeric and garam masala powder, green chilies and let simmer for 5 minutes.
5. Add the peas, and cook until peas are tender, then add paneer, reduce heat and simmer until sauce is thickened. Swirl the heavy cream in and garnish with fresh cilantro and mint, serve immediately.

Masala Green Beans

Prep Time: 20 minutes

Servings: 4

Ingredients:

75g onion
3 large cloves garlic, finely chopped
1 tsp ground cumin
1 tsp ground coriander
1 tsp sweet paprika
½ tsp red chili pepper flakes
¾ tsp salt
180ml coconut milk
1. 2 kilo green beans, trimmed and cut into 1-inch pieces
Juice of ½ a lime
2 tbsp chopped cilantro

Method:

1. In a medium pan over medium-high heat cook spices until fragrant, then set aside.
2. Heat oil in a pan and add onion and garlic, cook until soft and starting to turn light brown.
3. Add toasted spices, coconut milk and green beans, reduce heat and simmer gently for 15-20 minutes until beans are tender. Squeeze fresh lime juice on beans and garnish with fresh cilantro.

Split Yellow Dhal

Prep Time: 30 minutes

Servings: 4

Ingredients:

190g yellow split peas (channa dhal)
475ml water
1 onion, chopped
1 tbsp ghee
1 tsp turmeric
¼ tsp cayenne
½ tsp salt
1½ tsp cumin seeds
2 whole cloves
½ tsp of crushed garlic
1 tsp of chopped ginger
1 green chili, chopped
Salt
Fresh cracked black pepper

Method:

1. Rinse the peas and put in a large pot with water, turmeric, cayenne and salt. Simmer covered over low-medium heat for 20 minutes.
2. In a sauté pan over medium heat add the ghee, onion, cumin and clove, cook until onion is soft. Add garlic, ginger and green chili.
3. Add the onion and spices to the split peas, and simmer for 10 minutes.
4. Adjust seasoning with salt and pepper to taste.

Chickpea Dhal

Prep Time: 25 minutes

Servings: 4

Ingredients:

300g tomatoes
225g onion
2 cans chickpeas, drained and rinsed
2 tbsp fresh ginger, chopped
½ tsp of crushed garlic
1 green chili, chopped
2 tbsp ghee
Salt
½ tsp of black mustard seeds
½ tsp garam masala
1½ -2 tbsp curry powder
½ tsp of lemon juice

Method:

1. In a food processor or blender grind tomatoes, onion, chili, garlic and ginger until smooth.
2. In a medium sized skillet add ghee and black mustard seeds. Once seeds have popped add puree, curry powder, garam masala, cook over medium-low heat for 10 minutes.
3. Add chickpeas and continue to cook for 10 minutes.
4. Add salt and lemon juice to taste.

Black Eye Beans

Prep Time: 50 minutes (plus soaking time 8 hrs)

Servings: 4

Ingredients:

300g black eye beans
1 onion, chopped
2 tomatoes chopped
1 tbsp garlic, chopped
1 tbsp grated ginger
2 tbsp ghee
1½ tsp cumin powder
1 tsp of coriander powder
1½ tsp turmeric powder
½ tsp garam masala
1 tsp cumin seeds
2 dried red chilies, broken into small pieces
3 tbsp cilantro
1 tsp salt

Method:

1. Soak black-eyed beans 6-8 hours.
2. Cook in water with salt until they are soft and tender.
3. In a medium sized pan over medium-high heat add the cumin seeds and dry red chilies Cook until the cumin seeds start to splutter, add the onions, garlic and ginger, cook until onions are soft.
4. Add the tomatoes and mash them as they cook so they become a thick paste.
5. Add all the spices - the turmeric powder, coriander powder, cumin seeds and garam masala and simmer for about 5-8 minutes.
6. Add the black eye beans and simmer for another 5-8 minutes.
7. Add salt to taste and garnish with fresh cilantro.

VEGETABLE AND LENTIL CURRIES

Potato with Cauliflower

Prep Time: 30 minutes

Servings: 4

Ingredients:

1 cauliflower, cut into small florets
1 russet potato, peeled and cut into ½-inch cubes (similar size to cauliflower)
2 tbsp ginger
2 tbsp garlic
1 tbsp ground coriander
¼ tsp turmeric
240ml coconut milk, divided
2 tbsp oil
1 large serrano pepper, split down the middle leaving halves attached
1 tsp cumin seeds
Salt
2 tbsp cilantro leaves

Method:

1. Blend the ginger, garlic, coriander, turmeric, and 125ml coconut milk in blender to make a wet masala, set aside.
2. In a large pot, over medium-high heat add oil, serrano pepper, wait 30 seconds, and then add the cumin seeds and wait until they're done spluttering. Carefully add the wet masala. Cook until the paste thickens and deepens in color slightly.
3. Add the cauliflower and potatoes, Season with salt and add the remainder of the coconut milk. Cover and cook over medium heat 10 to 15 minutes.
4. Garnish with cilantro and serve immediately.

Spinach Saag

Prep Time: 15 minutes

Servings: 4

Ingredients:

1 box frozen spinach or fresh
2 tbsp oil
1 onion, chopped
2 tomatoes, chopped
1 tsp garlic chopped
1 tsp ginger, grated
½ tsp ground cumin
½ tsp ground coriander
¼ tsp turmeric powder
¼ tsp red chili powder
120ml plain yogurt

Method:

1. Cook spinach until almost all of the water has boiled out, then blend in a food processor or blender to make a puree, set aside.
2. In a pan over medium heat add oil and onions cook until golden. Add tomatoes, ginger and garlic. Mix well, add dry seasoning. Stir until it thickens.
3. Add spinach, mix well. Simmer for 3-4 minutes, remove from heat, add plain yogurt. Serve immediately

VEGETABLE AND LENTIL CURRIES

Carrots Peas & Potatoes

Prep Time: 30 minutes

Servings: 4

Ingredients:

1 packet of frozen mixed peas and carrots
4 potatoes, diced
1 onion, chopped
1 tbsp ground cumin
1 tsp ground turmeric
1 tbsp ground coriander
1 tsp chili powder
½ tsp salt
1 tbsp oil
120ml water

Method:

1. In a large skillet over medium-high heat add oil, onion, cumin, turmeric, coriander, chili powder and salt, cook until onion is browned.
2. Reduce the heat to medium, and stir in the potatoes, carrots and peas, add water as needed. Stir well then cover and cook until potatoes are tender, about 20 minutes.

Eggplant

Prep Time: 50 minutes

Servings: 4

Ingredients:

1 eggplant, peeled and chopped
1 onion, sliced
1 large tomato - peeled, seeded and diced
2tbsp vegetable oil
½tsp cumin seeds
1tsp ginger, grated
1 clove garlic, minced
½tsp ground turmeric
½tsp ground cumin
½tsp ground coriander
¼tsp cayenne pepper
Salt
Fresh ground black pepper to taste
3tbsp chopped fresh cilantro

Method:

1. Preheat oven to 180 °C/ 350°F
2. Toss eggplant in oil and roast in oven for 15-20 minutes until soft.
3. In a large pan over medium heat, heat the oil and add cumin seeds cook until golden brown. Add the onion, ginger and garlic, cook and stir until tender.
4. Add tomato, turmeric, ground cumin, ground coriander, cayenne pepper, salt and black pepper.
5. Add eggplant pieces and simmer for 15 minutes, adjust salt and pepper to taste.
6. Garnish with cilantro. Serve immediately.

VEGETABLE AND LENTIL CURRIES

Okra

Prep Time: 25 minutes

Servings: 2

Ingredients:

1 pound okra, sliced
3tbsp ghee
1 onion, chopped
½ tsp ground cumin
½ tsp ground ginger
½ tsp ground coriander
¼ tsp chili
¼ tsp turmeric
Salt

Method:

1. In a large skillet over medium heat add the ghee and onion, cook until tender.
2. Add the okra, cumin, ginger, coriander, chili, turmeric and salt to taste. Cook and stir to combine seasoning, then reduce the heat to low and cover the pan. Cook until okra is tender and the Okra is no longer sticky, should take about 15-20 minutes. (Okra releases a stickiness which needs to be cooked out.)

Spinach with Paneer

Prep Time: 40 minutes

Servings: 2

Ingredients:

400g baby spinach, cleaned and chopped
1 onion, chopped
¼ tsp cinnamon
¼ tsp ground cardamom
1 tsp ground ginger
½ tsp chopped garlic
½ cup chopped tomato
3 tbsp plain yogurt
1 tbsp coriander powder
½ tsp garam masala
½ tsp paprika
½ tsp salt
1 tbsp oil
230g paneer cheese, cut into cubes
120ml double cream

Method:

1. In a large skillet over medium heat add oil, onion, cinnamon, cardamom, and ginger and cook until onion is translucent.
2. Add garlic, chopped tomatoes and spinach then reduce heat.
3. Add coriander, garam masala, paprika, and salt to taste, stir well to combine, reduce heat and simmer for approximately 25-30 minutes.
4. Remove from heat and puree ½ the mixture in food processor or blender, return to skillet and stir. Slowly add double cream, and paneer cubes and heat through on a very low heat.

VEGETABLE AND LENTIL CURRIES

Red Kidney Beans

Prep Time: 60 minutes (plus soaking 8 hrs for beans)

Servings: 4

Ingredients:

240g red kidney beans soaked in water 6-8 hours
2 onions pureed
3 tomatoes pureed
Asafoetida - pinch
2 bay leaves
1 tbsp ginger, grated
1 tbsp garlic, chopped
¼ tsp turmeric
1 tsp red chili flakes
1 tbsp coriander powder
½ tsp cumin powder
½ tsp kasuri methi
2 tsp garam masala powder
3 tbsp oil
1 tsp cumin seeds
2 tbsp ghee
Salt
Fresh coriander leaves for garnish (optional)

Method:

1. Cook beans until soft in water with 1tsp of salt.
2. In a large skillet over medium heat add, ghee, oil, cumin seeds and bay leaf and allow the seeds to splutter. Add the asafoetida then add the ground onion paste and cook until golden brown.
3. Add the red chili flakes, turmeric, coriander, cumin, kasuri methi,

garam masala and salt to taste. Mix well.
4. Add the tomato puree and cook till oil separates.
5. Add the cooked kidney beans and some of the water they were cooked in.
6. Blend up to ½ cup of this mixture to create a gravy consistency. Simmer covered for 10-12 minutes.
7. Garnish with coriander leaves.

Snacks

Bhel Puri

Prep Time: 30 minutes

Servings: 4

Ingredients:

420g puffed rice
70g roasted and salted peanuts
2 potatoes boiled, peeled and chopped into tiny cubes
1 onion chopped fine
1 tomato chopped fine
1 bunch cilantro, chopped fine
2 green chilies chopped fine
Tamarind chutney
Mint chutney
100g Sev (vermicelli-like snack made from gram flour (gluten free) and available at Indian stores)

Method:

1. In a large bowl combine puffed rice, sev, peanuts, potato, onion, tomato, cilantro and green chilies, mix very well.
2. According to your own taste preferences, garnish with papdi, tamarind or mint chutney, serve and eat immediately. (refer to papdi chat recipe for on how to make papdi)

Spicy Gluten Free Crackers

Prep Time: 40 minutes

Servings: 4

Ingredients:

60g chickpea flour, sifted before measuring
¼tsp salt
¼tsp baking powder
1/8 tsp turmeric
2 tbsp nutritional yeast
½tsp oil
2-4 tbsp water
For dusting: gluten-free baking flour
Smoked spanish paprika

Method:

1. Pre heat the oven to 180 °C/ 350°F.
2. Sift dry ingredients together in a medium sized bowl. Add the oil and the water one tablespoon at a time. When the dough forms a ball, you have added enough water.
3. Knead the dough for 3-4 minutes, wrap in plastic and let rest for 15 minutes.
4. Dust your work area and rolling pin well with the gluten-free flour.
5. Divide the dough in half and roll it out until it is as thin as you can get it and still be able to pick it up.
6. Use a sharp knife or a cookie cutter to cut the dough into cracker shapes
7. Place the dough onto a baking sheet and dock each cracker twice with a fork, sprinkle with the paprika.
8. Bake until crispy 12-16 minutes, cool completely before serving.

Sabudana Vada

Prep Time: 30 minutes (soaking time up to 8hrs)

Servings: 4

Ingredients:

140g Tapioca pearls, soaked in water for 4-6 hours, until soft
4 medium potatoes peeled, boiled and mashed
½ cup peanuts
1 tsp cumin seeds
2 green chilies, chopped
1 tsp ginger grated
Juice of ½ of a lemon
1 tbsp chopped coriander leaves
2 tsp sugar
Rock salt
Vegetable oil for frying

Method:

1. Mix the mashed potatoes and tapioca together.
2. In a dry skillet over medium heat roast the peanuts till they become crisp. Cool and coarsely grind in a mortar & pestle or in a dry grinder.
3. In a small bowl mix together peanuts, rock salt, sugar, ginger, green chilies, coriander leaves and lemon juice.
4. Combine potato and tapioca mixture together with seasonings. Using a ¼cup portion of this mixture shape into small patties, until all the mixture is gone.
4. Heat vegetable oil to 190 °C/ 375°F and deep-fry the sabudana vadas until golden brown.
5. Drain onto paper towels and serve immediately with chutney of your choice.

… SNACKS

Poppadums

Prep Time: 240 minutes

Servings: 4

Ingredients:

240g garbanzo bean flour
1 tsp black pepper, coarse ground
1 tsp cumin
½ tsp salt
1 garlic clove, minced
60ml water
1 tbsp water
1 tbsp cayenne pepper
120ml vegetable oil

Method:

1. Preheat oven to 170 °C/ 325°F.
2. Combine the garbanzo bean flour, black pepper, cumin and salt and pulse in a food processor or mix vigorously by hand, add garlic and pulse.
3. Slowly add the water until the dough forms a ball. The dough needs to be stiff and dry.
4. Using your hands roll the dough into a 6-inch log, cut into ½ inch slices. Brush each round with oil and roll into thin circles about 6 inches in diameter.
5. Place on a baking sheet sprayed with pan spray, and bake until dry about 15-18 minutes.
6. Let poppadoms cool and continue to dry on the counter for 2-3 hours before frying in a heavy skillet over medium high heat, drain on paper towels and serve immediately.

Bhakri

Prep Time: 30 minutes

Servings: *4*

Ingredients:

240gms millet flour
4 tbsp ghee (and more for frying)
2 tsp sesame seeds
½ tsp red chili powder
½ tsp ginger, grated
Salt
Water (in small amounts)

Method:

1. Combine all the ingredients, add water a little at a time and knead into very firm dough. Cover and let rest for 15 minutes.
2. Divide the dough into 10 equal portions.
3. Roll out each portion into a 4 inch circles.
4. Heat a heavy skillet over medium high heat.
5. Cook the bhakris until golden brown on each side.

Spiced Nut Mix

Prep Time: 15 minutes

Servings: 4

Ingredients:

150g brazil nuts
150g almonds
150g peanuts
150g cashew nuts
2 tsp olive oil
2 tsp ground cumin
2 tsp ground coriander
2 tsp garam masala
1 tsp sweet paprika
1 tsp ground fennel
1 tsp ground turmeric
Salt
Freshly cracked black pepper
75g raisins

Method:

1. Preheat oven to 150 °C/ 300°F.
2. Combine the nuts and spices in a bowl with the olive oil. Season with salt and pepper. Place in a large roasting pan.
3. Roast in the oven for about 15 minutes, stirring frequently until nuts are toasted and aromatic.
4. Allow to cool completely and add raisins.

Lentil Spread

Prep Time: 40 minutes

Servings: 4

Ingredients:

140g lentils, soaked for an hour
1 tsp turmeric
475-500ml vegetable stock
2 tbsp oil
1 tsp cumin seeds
A generous pinch of asafotida
3 dry whole dried chili pepper
1 tbsp garlic, chopped
1 onion, diced
1 tbsp cilantro, chopped
Fresh lime wedges
1 tsp red crushed pepper
Chili oil
Salt

Method:

1. In a medium pot cook lentils with salt and turmeric until the lentils are soft and cooked thoroughly.
2. In a skillet over medium heat add oil and cook asafoetida, cumin seeds and the red chili peppers until the spices splutter and the chilies turn dark brown. Add the chopped garlic and onions and fry until the onions are medium brown.
3. Add the cooked lentils to the pan and stir well to combine. Simmer over low heat for about 20 minutes, until the liquid evaporates and the lentils are thick.
4. Cool completely. Garnish with fresh cilantro, lime wedges, crushed red pepper and chili oil.

Fish and Seafood

Spicy Coconut Shrimp

Prep Time: 30 minutes (plus marinate shrimps up to 2hrs)

Servings: 2

Ingredients:

½ kilo shrimp, peeled and deveined
350ml coconut milk
1 jalapeño pepper, sliced in half
1 tbsp garlic, chopped
2 tbsp ginger, grated
Juice from ½ a lime
1 tsp garam masala powder
2 tbsp vegetable oil
Salt fresh cracked pepper
45g coconut shavings, toasted
1 tbsp cilantro leaves
¼ tsp red chili flakes
Lime wedges

Method:

1. In a blender or food processor puree the coconut milk, jalapeño, garlic, ginger, garam masala, lime and oil and salt and pepper to taste.
2. Marinate the shrimp in the coconut milk mixture in a small bowl in the refrigerator for 1 to 2 hours.
3. Drain the shrimps but save the marinade and place it in a small saucepan, bring to a boil and reduce.
4. In a heavy skillet over medium high heat, add oil and shrimp, sauté until cooked through.
5. Add the marinade, stir well to combine.
6. Garnish with the toasted coconut, cilantro, chili flakes and lime wedges. Serve immediately.

FISH AND SEAFOOD

Fish Cakes

Prep Time: 40 minutes

Servings: 2

Ingredients:

340g potatoes, peeled & cubed
340g boneless skinless salmon fillets, cubed
75g onion, chopped
2 small red chilies, chopped
2 tsp garlic chopped
1 tbsp ginger, grated
1 tsp turmeric
1 tsp paprika
2 tsp chili paste
1-2 red onions, finely sliced
Juice of 1 lemon
1 egg
Salt
Vegetable oil

Method:

1. In a medium sized pot boil potatoes in water until tender, drain and set aside.
2. Heat a little oil in a heavy-bottomed pan and gently sauté the onion, chilies, garlic, ginger, turmeric, paprika and the chili paste, regularly stirring, until the onion is cooked.
3. Add salmon and mix well, add 2 tablespoons of water, cover the pan and reduce heat. Cook until salmon is done about 8-10 minutes.
4. Combine potatoes and salmon mixture adding the egg and lemon

juice. Form about 6-8 round and slightly flattened patties.
5. Sauté the patties in a skillet with oil over medium high heat until browned on each side.
6. Drain on paper towels and serve immediately.

Shrimp Balchao

Prep Time: 15 minutes

Servings: 2

Ingredients:

1/3 kilo shrimp, cleaned and deveined
1 onion, chopped
½ tsp turmeric powder
2 tbsp ginger, grated
1 tbsp garlic, chopped
1 tsp mustard seeds
10 Kashmiri red chilies, soaked in hot water
½ tsp cumin seeds
1 tsp sugar
120ml vinegar
2 tbsp tomato paste
Salt

Method:

1. In a saucepan over medium heat, heat oil and add the onions and cumin seeds. Cook onions until they are soft.
2. Combine the turmeric powder, ginger, garlic, mustard seeds, chilies, sugar, vinegar and tomato paste in a blender until pureed, to form masala paste.
3. Add the masala paste to the onions. Reduce heat and cook stirring continuously.
4. Add the shrimp and the salt. Cook until the shrimp are bright pink, about 6-8 minutes. Serve immediately.

Curried Halibut

Prep Time: 30 minutes

Servings: 2

Ingredients:

1 kilo skinless halibut fillets, cut into 4-inch pieces
2 tbsp oil
1 onion, minced
2 tbsp finely chopped fresh ginger
4 garlic cloves, minced
1 tsp cayenne pepper
1 tsp turmeric
1 tsp ground coriander
240ml plain whole-milk yogurt
240ml cream
1 tbsp garam masala
Pinch of saffron threads, crumbled
Salt

Method:

1. In large, deep skillet, heat the oil. Add the onion, ginger and garlic and cook over moderate heat, stirring frequently, until lightly browned, about 6 minutes.
2. Add the cayenne, turmeric and coriander and cook for 1 minute, stirring.
3. Whisk in the yogurt, then add the cream, garam masala and saffron and bring to a boil.
4. Reduce the heat and simmer the sauce until slightly thickened, about 10 minutes. Season with salt to your taste.
5. Add the halibut to the sauce, cook over medium heat, turning once, until the fish is cooked, about 8-12 minutes.

Fish with Red Curry

Prep Time: 20 minutes

Servings: 2

Ingredients:

½ kilo white fish fillets, cut into 2-inch pieces
2 tbsp vegetable oil
1 onion, sliced
1 zucchini, thinly sliced
1 red bell pepper, thinly sliced
30g fine rice flour
2 tbsp Thai red curry paste
350ml unsweetened coconut milk
2 tbsp fish sauce
3 tbsp cilantro, chopped

Method:

1. In a large skillet over medium heat add 1tbsp of oil, onion, zucchini and bell pepper. Cook, until vegetables are soft and lightly browned, 6-8 minutes.
2. Remove the vegetables to a plate.
3. Dredge the fish in the rice-flour.
4. Add 1 tbsp of oil to a large skillet over medium high heat. When the oil is hot, add the fish, fry, turning once, until golden brown, 2-3 minutes per side.
5. Remove the fish to the vegetable plate.
6. Heat the curry paste in the same pan, then pour in the coconut milk, fish sauce and half of the cilantro. Add the vegetables and fish back in. Bring the liquid to a simmer over medium-low heat and cook, until the fish is cooked through and the vegetables are hot, 4-6 minutes.
7. Stir in the rest of the cilantro and serve immediately.

Tandoori Fish

Prep Time: 20 minutes (plus marinate for 3hrs)

Servings: 4

Ingredients:

1 kilo thick cod, cut into large pieces
80ml vinegar
4 cloves garlic
1 tbsp chopped fresh ginger
½ tsp salt
1 tbsp cayenne pepper
1 tbsp ground coriander
1 tbsp ground cumin
120ml vegetable oil

Method:

1. Blend the vinegar, garlic, ginger, salt, cayenne, coriander, cumin, and oil in a blender to make a thick sauce.
2. Brush the fish chunks with the sauce to coat evenly and place in a shallow dish, marinate in the refrigerator for 3 hours.
3. Preheat the oven's broiler. Arrange the marinated fish in a broiler-safe dish, reserving the extra marinade.
4. Broil the fish under the preheated broiler on the oven's center rack for 9-12 minutes on each side. Brush the fish with extra marinade. Cook until the fish flakes easily with a fork, serve immediately.

Fish & Tomato Curry

Prep Time: 30 minutes

Servings: 2

Ingredients:

½ kilo of Pollack fillets, cut into medium sized pieces
3 tbsp oil
1 onion, thinly sliced
8 tomatoes, roughly chopped
1 tbsp garlic cloves
1 tbsp ginger, grated
1 tbsp garam masala
350ml coconut milk
3 tbsp cilantro, chopped

Method:

1. In a large skillet over medium heat, add 2 tbsp oil and onions, cook until onions are soft.
2. Blend the tomatoes, garlic and ginger in a blender until smooth. Add the garam masala to the onions and cook for 2 minutes.
3. Add the tomato mix and simmer for 8-10 minutes until thickened. Add the coconut milk and simmer over low heat.
4. Season the fish fillets with salt.
5. In a medium sized skillet heat 1tbsp oil and sauté the fillets, until golden brown and cooked through, about 6 minutes each side.
6. Set the fish in the tomato curry and cook for 4-6 minutes to combine flavors, garnish with cilantro and serve immediately.

Coconut Lime Fish

Prep Time: 15 minutes

Servings: 2

Ingredients:

½ kilo tilapia fillets
90g unsweetened shredded coconut
2 tbsp lime zest
2 tbsp cilantro, chopped
1 tsp red chilli flakes
2 eggs
Salt
Fresh cracked black pepper

Method:

1. Preheat oven to 190 °C/ 375°F.
2. Combine the coconut, lime zest, cilantro and chilli flakes, salt and pepper.
3. Beat the eggs. Dip the fish in the egg then dredge in coconut, place on a non-stick baking sheet lightly sprayed with pan spray. Bake until golden and cooked through about 20 minutes, turning once.

Egg, Chicken and Lamb

Egg Masala with Potatoes

Prep Time: 30 minutes

Servings: 4

Ingredients:

6 eggs, boiled and peeled
2 large potatoes, peeled and chopped
1 sized onion, chopped
1 green chilli, seeded and chopped
1 tsp garlic, chopped
1 tsp ginger, grated
1 tsp ground cumin
1 tsp ground turmeric
1 tsp chilli powder
2 tbsp tomato paste
2 tbsp ghee
475ml vegetable stock
Salt

Method:

1. In a pot over medium-high heat add ghee, onions and potatoes, cook until potatoes and onions begin to brown 8-10 minutes. Reduce heat and add all the spices plus ginger, garlic and tomato paste, stir well to combine.
2. Add vegetable stock to cover potatoes, and simmer until potatoes are soft, then add salt and eggs.
3. Add more vegetable stock if needed to cover eggs, simmer for 10 minutes. Serve immediately.

Curried Eggs with Raita

Prep Time: 10 minutes

Servings: 4

Ingredients:

6 eggs
60ml cream
1 tsp yellow curry
¼ tsp red chilli flakes
1 tbsp ghee
½ tsp garlic, chopped
½ tsp ginger, grated
Salt
120ml raita
2 tbsp cilantro leaves, chopped

Method:

1. Beat eggs very well with cream.
2. Heat a large skillet over medium high heat and add ghee. Once ghee is hot add yellow curry, chili flakes, garlic and ginger, cook for 1 minute.
3. Add eggs mixture. Stir the eggs constantly while cooking until set.
4. Garnish with raita and cilantro. Serve immediately.

Eggs Poached in Tomato Chili Sauce

Prep Time: 20 minutes

Servings: 4

Ingredients:

6 eggs
½ onion, chopped
1 tsp garlic, chopped
1 hot green chillies chopped
1 mild green chilli; chopped into rings
½ red pepper chopped
4 tomatoes, chopped
1 tbsp red curry paste
1 tbsp oil
120ml coconut milk
120ml vegetable stock
Salt

Method:

1. In a medium sized skillet over medium heat add oil, onion, garlic, both chillis, peppers, tomatoes and red curry paste, cook until vegetables are soft and tomatoes are mushy.
2. Add coconut milk and vegetable stock, stir to combine and cook until hot, add salt to taste.
3. Crack eggs into the curry, reduce heat and simmer until eggs are poached 6-9 minutes. Serve immediately.

Chick Peas and Spinach with Chicken

Prep Time: 80 minutes

Servings: 4

Ingredients:

6 bone-in chicken legs (thigh and drumstick), skin removed
1 can chickpeas, rinsed
240g baby spinach
2 onions, sliced
1 tbsp garlic, chopped
1 tbsp ginger, grated
2 green chilies, chopped
4 tbsp oil
2 tsp ground coriander
2 tsp ground cumin
2 tsp ground turmeric
¼ tsp cayenne pepper
375ml water
Salt
3 tbsp cilantro, chopped

Method:

1. Preheat to 190°C / 375°F
2. Heat a large roasting pan over medium high heat, add 2 tbsp oil and brown chicken on both sides, cooking for about 6-8 minutes each side, set chicken aside.
3. Add remaining 2tbsp of oil and onions to the drippings in the roasting pan, reduce heat to medium. Cook onions until soft, season with salt. Add garlic, ginger, chillis coriander, cumin, turmeric, and cayenne. Cook until spices are fragrant.

4. Stir in chickpeas, spinach and some water.
5. Add chicken, use more water if needed to cover chicken about three-fourths of the way up. Bring to a simmer, cover and put in the oven.
6. Braise chicken for 60 minutes until meat is very tender and almost ready to fall off the bone. Serve immediately.

Chicken with Cardamom

Prep Time: 60 minutes

Servings: 4

Ingredients:

1 kilo skin-on, bone-in chicken thighs
3 tbsp raisins
4 tbsp ghee
2 onions, thinly sliced
Salt
Freshly ground black pepper
10 cardamom pods
¼ tsp whole cloves
2 cinnamon sticks
285g basmati rice
375ml chicken stock
3 tbsp cilantro, chopped

Method:

1. Heat a large pot over medium high heat, add 2 tbsp ghee and brown chicken on both sides cooking for about 6-8 minutes each side, set chicken aside.
2. Add remaining ghee and onions to pot, cook until onions begin to brown, add spices and rice stirring well to coat the rice with ghee.
3. Add chicken back to the pot and cover with chicken stock, cover pot, reduce to a simmer and cook for 35-40 minutes (adding more chicken stock if needed).
4. When rice is tender, turn off heat, add raisins and let sit for 10 minutes.
5. Fluff rice, garnish with cilantro.

Roasted Chicken

Prep Time: 110 minutes

Servings: 4-6

Ingredients:

One 2.25 kilo chicken, rinsed and dried
Salt
Fresh cracked black pepper
Juice of 1 lemon
2 tbsp garam masala
1 tbsp ground cardamom
1 tbsp smoked paprika
1 tsp turmeric
½ tsp ground cinnamon
3 tbsps oil
350ml water

Method:

1. Preheat the oven 190 °C/ 375°F.
2. Mix together the oil, lemon juice and spices.
3. Pour mixture over the chicken and into the cavity, massage it into the meat with your hands. Season chicken with salt and pepper as well.
4. Place the chicken in a roasting pan, add the water and place in the oven, roast for 25 minutes then reduce heat to 150 °C/ 300°F, cover chicken loosely with foil and cook until juices run clear for a further 60 minutes.
5. Allow chicken to rest for 15 minutes before carving.

EGG, CHICKEN AND LAMB

Butter Chicken

Prep Time: 70 minutes (plus marinating 1hr)

Servings: 4

Ingredients:

1 kilo boneless skinless chicken, chopped
Juice of 1 lime
Salt
1 tsp red chilli powder
6 cloves
8-10 peppercorns
3 sticks of cinnamon
4 bay leaves
8-10 almonds
10 cardamom seeds
240ml yogurt
3 tbsp vegetable oil
2 onions chopped
2 tsp garlic chopped
1 tsp ginger grated
2 tsp coriander powder
1 tsp cumin powder
¼ tsp turmeric powder
6 tomatoes, pureed in blender
375ml water
3 tbsp butter, melted
Salt

Method:

1. Marinate the chicken in lime juice, salt and red chilli powder in a

large, non-metallic bowl for 1 hour.
2. In a small skillet over medium heat gently cook the cloves, peppercorns, cinnamon, bay leaves and almonds till they darken slightly.
3. Cool the mixture and add the cardamom seeds.
4. Grind the mixture into a coarse powder in a clean, dry coffee grinder.
5. Mix the yoghurt into the spice powder you have ground. Then add coriander, cumin and turmeric powders together.
6. Mix the yoghurt mixture to the chicken and allow to marinate for an hour.
7. In a large skillet over medium heat add vegetable oil and onions. Cook until golden then add garlic and ginger. Remove chicken from marinade and add chicken pieces to the skillet, stir frequently and cook for 8-10 minutes.
8. Add the tomato puree, water, and left over marinade, reduce heat and simmer gently for 35-40 minutes.
9. Allow to sit for 10 minutes, add melted butter and serve immediately.

Fried Chicken Masala

Prep Time: 50 minutes (plus 6-8 hours marinade time)

Servings: 6-8

Ingredients:

2.25 kilo of chicken pieces
375ml yogurt
4 tsp garam masala
2 tsp ground turmeric
3 tsp ground coriander
1 tsp ground black pepper
½ tsp ginger, grated
½ tsp ground cayenne pepper
230g millet flour
230g gram flour
½ tsp salt
Vegetable oil for frying

Method:

1. Marinate chicken for 6-8 hours in the refrigerator in yogurt, 2tsp garam masala, 1tsp turmeric, 1tsp coriander, black pepper, ginger and 1/4 cayenne.
2. Lay chicken out for 20 minutes before frying.
3. Heat vegetable oil in a large heavy skillet to 180 °C/ 350°F.
4. In a big bowl combine millet flour, gram flour, 2tsp coriander, 2tsp garam masala, 2tsp turmeric, salt, ¼ tsp cayenne.
5. Dredge chicken in seasoned flour and fry in batches in hot oil until browned and cooked through. Serve immediately.

Tandoori Chicken

Prep Time: 50 minutes (plus 6-8 hours marinade time)

Servings: 4

Ingredients:

1 kilo chicken breast, cut into 4 oz pieces
240ml plain yogurt
2 tbsp lemon juice
4 minced garlic cloves
2 tbsp minced fresh ginger
1 tsp salt
1 tsp ground coriander
1 tsp ground cumin
1 tsp ground turmeric
1 tsp cayenne
1 tbsp garam masala
1 tbsp sweet paprika

Method:

1. Heat a small pan over medium heat, add oil and spices, cook until fragrant. Then remove from heat and cool.
2. Combine the spice mixture with the yogurt, lemon juice, garlic, ginger and salt.
3. Marinate the chicken in the yogurt for 6-8 hours leave in refrigeration.
4. Preheat oven to 190 °C/ 375°F.
5. Heat a grill pan on medium-high heat and brush with oil. Remove chicken from marinade, allowing excess to drip off.
6. Sear chicken until outside is browned and just a little black. Remove to a roasting pan and let finish cooking in the oven for 20-

25 minutes until the juices run clear.
7. Let rest for 10 minutes before serving.

Chicken Coriander

Prep Time: 45 minutes

Servings: 4

Ingredients:

1 whole Chicken quartered
1 tbsp garlic, chopped
1 tbsp ginger, grated
1 tbsp coriander seeds
1 tbsp garam masala
2 tbsp ghee
2 tbsp tomato paste
700ml chicken stock
1 bunch chopped fresh cilantro
240ml crushed tomatoes
Salt
Fresh cracked black pepper

Method:

1. In a large skillet over medium heat add ghee, garlic, ginger, coriander seeds, garam masala, cook until spices are fragrant.
2. Add tomato paste and the chicken pieces, season with salt and pepper.
3. Cook until chicken is golden about 6-8 minutes on each side.
4. Add chicken stock, crushed tomatoes and cilantro, reduce heat and simmer gently for 30-35 minutes.

Lamb Haleem

Prep Time: 160 minutes (plus 6-8hrs soaking for dhals)

Servings: 4

Ingredients:

95g urad dhal
95g yellow split peas
95g mung dhal
1 kilo lamb chump chops
2 tbsp garlic, chopped
2 tsp ginger, grated
2 tbsp ghee
¼ tsp saffron threads
1 tbsp ground coriander
1 tbsp ground cumin
1 tbsp chaat masala
1 tbsp ground chilli
1 tsp ground turmeric
3 tbsp coriander, chopped
3 tbsp mint leaves, chopped
1 long green chilli, sliced
1 lemon, cut into wedges
2 tbsp ghee
2 onions, thinly sliced

Method:

1. Soak dhals together for 6-8 hours, rinse.
2. Place dahls in a large heavy pot along with lamb, garlic and ginger, cover with 6 cups of water. Bring to a boil, reduce heat and simmer gently for 2 hours or until lamb is very tender. Remove lamb to a

large plate, reserving dhal in cooking liquid.
3. When lamb is cool enough to handle, remove bones from lamb and discard. Chop lamb and set aside.
4. In a large saucepan over medium heat add ghee, saffron and spices, and cook until fragrant. Add reserved dhal mixture and lamb. Reduce heat to low and cook, stirring occasionally, for 10 minutes or until heated through.
5. To make fried onions, heat ghee in a frying pan over medium heat. Add onions and cook, stirring occasionally, for 10-12 minutes or until golden.
6. Serve haleem immediately garnished with fried onions, coriander, mint, chilli, and lemon wedges.

Lamb Gosht

Prep Time: 60 minutes (plus 1 hour marinade time)

Servings: 4

Ingredients:

1 kilo boneless leg of lamb, cubed
240ml yogurt
1 tsp turmeric powder
3 tbsp garlic
3 tbsp ginger, grated
2 green chillies chopped
3 tbsp ghee
2 onions, sliced
3 tbsp garam masala
3 tsp coriander powder
3 tsp cumin powder
4 bay leaves
300g crushed tomatoes
475ml lamb stock (chicken stock if lamb is unavailable)
Freshly ground pepper
Salt
3 tbsp finely chopped mint leaves
3 tbsp finely chopped coriander leaves
2 cm piece of ginger, julienned

Method:

1. Season the lamb with salt & pepper then marinate in yogurt, turmeric powder, half the ginger and garlic pastes and green chillies for 1 hour.
2. In a large skillet over medium heat add ghee and onions cook until

onions are soft. Add tomatoes and remaining ginger and garlic pastes cook until fragrant.
3. Add cumin powder, bay leaves, coriander powder, garam masala and cook for 8-10 minutes.
4. Add the marinated lamb and stock, reduce heat to low and simmer for 35-40 minutes
5. Serve immediately garnished with chopped coriander, mint and juliennes of ginger.

Tandoori Lamb

Prep Time: 50 minutes (plus 6-8 hours marinade time)

Servings: 4

Ingredients:

8 lamb chops
275ml yogurt
120ml cream
Juice of ½ lemon
1 tbsp ginger, grated
1 tbsp garlic, chopped
1 tbsp garam masala
1 tbsp ground cumin
1 tbsp paprika
½ tsp cayenne pepper
¼ tsp freshly grated nutmeg
Salt
2 tbsp vegetable oil
3 tbsp unsalted butter, melted

Method:

1. Use a sharp knife and cut ¼ inch deep slashes in each lamb chop. Marinate chops in the yogurt, heavy cream, lemon juice, ginger, garlic, garam masala, cumin, paprika, cayenne, nutmeg and 1tsp of salt for 6- 8 hours.
2. Remove the chops from the marinade and let stand at room temperature for 30 minutes. Drizzle with oil.
3. Light the grill and heat to medium high heat. Grill for 6-8 minutes on each side, until well browned. Serve immediately.

Roti, Nans, Paratha and Teplas

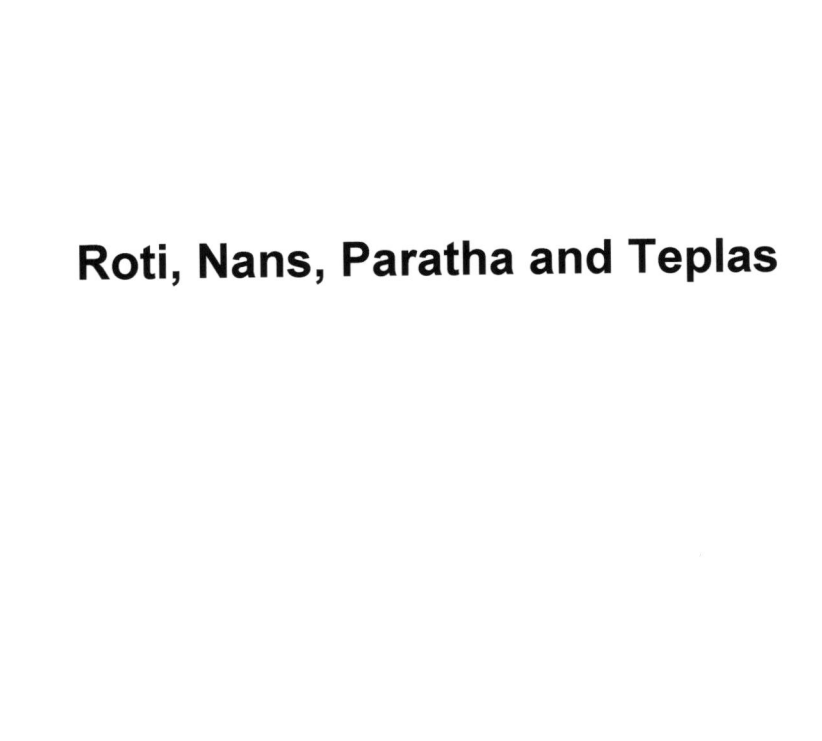

Gluten Free Roti

Prep Time: 40 minutes

Servings: 4

Ingredients:

240g millet flour
1 tsp salt
1½ tbsp vegetable oil
Warm water

Method:

1. Combine flour and salt in a large bowl, mix in oil and add water slowly to form a soft dough. Coat the dough with oil and let it rest for 20 minutes.
2. Knead the dough for 3 minutes and then form into small balls. Roll the dough balls out into thin round discs (about 6 inch wide), using extra millet flour to prevent sticking. (If it does stick roll discs on a plastic food bag.)
3. Heat a large heavy skillet over medium-high heat, add a few drops of oil, cook roti for a minute on each side. Keep rotis in warm oven and brush liberally with ghee.

Savory Gluten Free Paratha

Prep Time: 20 minutes

Servings: 4

Ingredients:

240g millet flour
1 tsp salt
1½ tbsp vegetable oil
Warm water
150g potatoes, cooked and chopped
1 tsp garlic, chopped
1 hot chilli, chopped
3 tbsp green onion sliced
½ tsp cayenne
1 tsp cumin
3 tbsp cilantro

Method:

1. Combine flour and salt in a large bowl, mix in oil and add water slowly to form a soft dough. Coat the dough with oil and let it rest for 20 minutes.
2. Mash potatoes, garlic, chilli, green onions, cayenne, cumin and cilantro together in a bowl. Knead potato mixture into the dough for 2-3 minutes and then form into small balls. Roll the dough balls out into thin round discs,(about 6 inch wide) using extra millet flour to prevent sticking.
3. In a large heavy skillet over medium-high heat, add a few drops of oil, cook paratha for a minute on each side. Keep paratha in warm oven and brush liberally with ghee.

Gluten Free Methi Teplas

Prep Time: 40 minutes

Servings: 4

Ingredients:

120g chickpea flour
120g juwar flour
1/8 tsp asafetida
½ tsp cumin seeds
½ tsp turmeric
1 tsp red chili flakes
1 tsp salt
3 tbsp fenugreek leaves
2 tbsp oil
120ml yogurt
Water as needed
Vegetable oil for cooking

Method:

1. In a bowl, combine all dry ingredients - chickpea flour, juwar flour, asafetida, cumin seeds, turmeric, chili flakes, salt, and fenugreek leaves.
2. Add oil and yogurt to the dry ingredients and mix well. Add water as needed to make firm dough.
3. Knead the dough for 2 minutes to make smooth and pliable dough.
4. Cover the dough with a damp cloth and let rest for ten minutes. Divide the dough into 8 equal pieces and roll into a 6 inch disk.
5. Heat a large heavy skillet on medium high. Lightly oil the skillet, and cook the teplas in the pan until the dough is golden brown, flip and cook on the other side.

Sweet Gluten Free Naan with Raisins & Nuts

Prep Time: 30 minutes

Servings: 4

Ingredients:

60g millet flour
60g chickpea flour
60g almond flour
1 tsp baking powder
1 tsp baking soda
1 tsp salt
1 tbsp sugar
½ tsp cinnamon
½ tsp ginger
½ tsp cardamom
2 tbsp ghee
Milk
30g Raisins, 30g almonds, 30g coconut mix, cooked in ghee.
30g coconut

Method:

1. In a large bowl combine all dry ingredients, add ghee and milk to make a smooth dough. Cover dough and let rest for 10 minutes. Add cooked raisins, nuts, and coconut, knead for 2 minutes, divide dough into 8-10 equal portions.
2. Roll into 4-6 inch disks.
3. Heat a heavy skillet over medium heat, and cook Naan until golden on each side, brush with ghee and garnish with coconut. Serve immediately.

Cauliflower Stuffed Paratha

Prep Time: 40 minutes

Servings: 4

Ingredients:

120g millet flour
60g chickpea flour
60g almond flour
1 tsp salt
1½ tbsp vegetable oil
Warm water
300g cauliflower, cooked and chopped
1 tbsp ghee
1 tsp garlic, chopped
1 tsp ginger, grated
1 hot chilli, chopped
3 tbsp green onion sliced
½ tsp cayenne
2 tsp yellow curry powder
¼ cup cilantro

Method:

1. Combine flours and salt in a large bowl, mix in oil and add water slowly to form a soft dough. Coat the dough with oil and let it rest for 20 minutes. Roll the dough balls out into thin round discs, using extra millet flour to prevent sticking.
2. In a skillet over medium heat cook cauliflower, garlic, ginger, chilli, green onions, cayenne, yellow curry powder and cilantro. Divide cauliflower mixture equally between paratha disks and fold disks over, and press edges to seal. (Half moon shape). Gently

flatten paratha with your hand.
3. In a large heavy skillet over medium-high heat, add a few drops of oil, cook paratha for a minute on each side. Keep paratha in warm oven and brush liberally with ghee.

Rice

Vegetable Biryana

Biryana is made in 2 parts and then each part is combined so the flavors can cook together. The ingredients are listed separately for each part.

Prep Time: 35 minutes

Servings: 4

Rice

Ingredients:

190g basmati rice
1 tbsp ghee
2 tbsp raisins
2 tbsp blanched, sliced almonds
½ tsp turmeric
¼ tsp whole cumin seeds
¼ tsp whole coriander seeds
3 whole cardamom pods
1 cinnamon stick, broken in half
475ml water
1 tsp salt

Vegetables

Ingredients:

2 tbsp unsalted butter
75g onion, thinly sliced
1 tbsp ginger, grated
1 tsp garlic, chopped
2 tbsp raisins

RICE

2 tbsp almonds, sliced
1 ½ tsp whole coriander seeds
½ tsp whole cumin seeds
5 whole cardamom pods
150g cauliflower florets
75g green beans, chopped
150g potatoes, peeled and chopped
1 carrot, chopped
Salt
180ml Water
2 tbsp toasted shredded coconut
2 tbsp, sliced almonds, toasted

Method:

1. Rinse the rice with water, set aside.
2. In a medium saucepan, over medium-high heat, add ghee, raisins, almonds, turmeric, cumin seed, coriander seed, cardamom pods, and cinnamon stick and cook, fragrant, about 3 minutes.
3. Add the rice and cook, stirring for 2 minutes more. Add the water and salt and bring to a boil. Lower the heat and simmer for 20 minutes. Remove from the heat and let rest, covered.
4. In a large skillet over medium heat add the butter, garlic and ginger until fragrant. Add raisins, almonds, coriander seed, cumin seed, and cardamom and cook until fragrant, about 2 minutes.
5. Add cauliflower, green beans, potatoes, carrots, and salt to taste. Increase heat to high add water and cook, reducing the water by half.
6. Combine the rice and vegetables, adjust salt to taste. Serve immediately garnishing with the toasted coconut and almonds.

Jeera Rice

Prep Time: 30 minutes

Servings: 4

Ingredients:

190g Basmati rice
700ml water
Salt
2 tbsp ghee
1 onion chopped
2 tsp cumin seeds
3 tbsp cilantro

Method:

1. Rinse the rice until the water runs clear, place in a medium sized pot on high heat.
2. Add water and salt to taste and bring to a boil. Cover and cook until rice is done, about 20 minutes.
3. In a small skillet over medium heat add ghee and onions. Cook until onions are golden brown and soft, add the cumin seeds, cook until the seeds splutter.
4. Add onions and cumin seeds to the rice and stir well.
5. Serve immediately garnished with cilantro.

Chicken Biryana

Biryana is made in 2 parts and then each part is combined so the flavors can cook together. The ingredients are listed separately for each part.

Prep Time: 85 minutes

Servings: 4

Chicken

Ingredients:

½ kilo boneless chicken. Skinless chicken pieces cut into chunks
2 potatoes, peeled and halved
2 large onions, finely chopped
2 tsp garlic, chopped
1 tbsp ginger, grated
½ tsp chili powder
½ tsp ground black pepper
½ tsp ground turmeric
1 tsp ground cumin
Salt
2 tomatoes, chopped
2 tbsp plain yogurt
2 tbsp chopped fresh mint leaves
½ tsp ground cardamom
240ml chicken stock
1 cinnamon stick

Rice

Ingredients:

2 ½ tbsp vegetable oil
1 onion, chopped
1 pinch powdered saffron
6 pods cardamom
4 whole cloves
1 cinnamon stick
½ tsp ginger, grated
1 pound basmati rice
1 liter water
1 ½ tsp salt

Method:

1. In a large skillet over medium heat, add onions and potatoes, cook until golden. Add garlic, ginger, chili, pepper, turmeric, cumin, salt and the tomatoes. Stir well to combine, cooking for 3-4 minutes.
2. Add yogurt, mint, cardamom and cinnamon stick reduce heat to low cover and cook for 10-12 minutes.
3. Add chicken pieces, stock and stir well, cover and cook for 30-35 more minutes.
4. Rinse the rice and drain.
5. In a large skillet add vegetable oil and onions cook until onions are soft. Add saffron, cardamom, cloves, cinnamon stick, ginger and rice. Stir to combine.
6. Add water and salt, bring to a boil, add chicken mixture, reduce heat and cook covered for 20 minutes or until rice is done. Serve immediately.

Peas Pillau

Prep Time: 30 minutes

Servings: 4

Ingredients:

150g peas
75g onion, chopped
1 green chilli chopped
1 tsp ginger, grated
4 cardamom pods
4 cloves
1 cinnamon stick
½ tsp turmeric
375ml water
2 tbsp ghee
190g basmati rice
Salt

Method:

1. Rinse the rice and drain.
2. In a large pot over low heat, add ghee, chilli, onion, ginger, cardamom, cloves, and cinnamon. Cook until the onions are soft, then add the rice. Stir well to combine.
3. Add peas, water and salt. Bring to a gentle boil, reduce heat to low and cook covered for 20 minutes or until the rice is done, serve immediately.

Sweet Rice with Raisins and Nuts

Prep Time: 40 minutes

Servings: 2

Ingredients:

1 cup brown basmati rice
2 tbsp ghee
1 tbsp ginger
½ cup onion, chopped
4 cloves
6 cardamom pods
1 cinnamon stick
375ml water
½ cup raisins
½ cup walnuts, toasted and chopped
2 tbsp mint
Salt
Freshly ground black pepper

Method:

1. In a medium saucepan over low heat, add ghee and onion, cook until onion is soft. Add ginger, cloves, cardamom, cinnamon and rice stir to combine.
2. Add water and salt, bring to a boil then reduce heat, cover and cook for 35 minutes or until the rice is done.
3. Add the raisins, nuts and mint, and salt and pepper to taste.

Carrot Rice

Prep Time: 35 minutes

Servings: 2

Ingredients:

1 cup basmati rice
375ml water
1 tbsp ghee
150g onion chopped
1 tsp ginger, grated
1 tsp garlic, chopped
150g carrots, grated
Salt
Cayenne pepper to taste
75g roasted peanuts
3 tbsp cilantro, chopped

Method:

1. In a medium saucepan over low heat add ghee, onions and carrots, cook until onion and carrots are tender.
2. Add ginger, garlic, cayenne, salt and rice, stir well to combine. Add water and bring to a boil, reduce heat cover and cook 20 minutes, until rice is done.
3. Garnish with peanuts and cilantro.

Desserts

Pistachio Kulfi

Prep Time: 20 minutes

Servings: 4

Ingredients:

1 liter whole milk
1 can sweetened condensed milk
100g powdered milk
100g sugar
1 tbsp vanilla extract
1 tsp cardamom powder
75g pistachios, chopped

Method:

1. In heavy saucepan combine all ingredients, except cardamon powder and pistachios, over medium low heat, stir constantly until the milk thickens and is reduced by 25%.
2. Remove from heat and add cardamom powder and pistachios, mixing well.
3. Cool completely pour into a freezer-safe container and freeze. When frozen, simply scoop and serve.

Gulab Jambu

Prep Time: 50 minutes

Servings: 4

Jambus

Ingredients:

100g dry milk powder
2 tbsp ghee
½ tsp baking powder
50ml warm milk
1 tbsp chopped almonds
1 tbsp chopped pistachio nuts
1/8 tsp cinnamon
1/8 tsp cardamom
Vegetable oil for deep frying

Rose Water Syrup

Ingredients:

200g sugar
240ml water
1 tsp rose water
1 pinch ground cardamom
1 pinch cinnamon
1 pinch nutmeg

Method:

1. In a saucepan, stir together the sugar, water, rose water, and the pinches of cardamom, cinnamon and nutmeg. Bring to a boil, and

simmer for 3-4 minutes. Set aside.
2. Combine the milk powder, baking powder, cinnamon and cardamom. Add the almonds, pistachios, melted ghee and milk, mix until well blended.
3. Cover and let rest for 15 minutes.
4. Knead the dough, and form into about 20 small balls.
5. Add vegetable oil to a large heavy skillet, heat oil to 180 °C/ 350°F degrees. Fry dough balls until they float and turn golden, drain on paper towels.
6. Add jambus to the rosewater syrup and simmer over low heat for 4-6 minutes. Serve immediately.

DESSERTS

Mango Lassi

Prep Time: 5 minutes

Servings: 2

Ingredients:

240ml yogurt
240ml milk
240ml mango puree
1 tbsp sugar
1/8 tsp cardamom
2 cubes of ice

Method:

1. Combine all ingredient in the blender and blend until smooth. Serve immediately

Carrot Halwa

Prep Time: 50 minutes

Servings: 4

Ingredients:

150g carrot grated
200g sugar
120ml ghee
1liter milk
Cashews
Pistachios
Raisins
Almonds

Method:

1. Garnish: 1 cups each Cashnuts, Pistachios, Raisins and Almonds chopped and fried in ghee.
2. In a small saucepan over medium heat add milk and bring to a boil, reduce heat. Let milk simmer for 25-30mins stirring continuously until it is reduced to a very thick cream. Remove from heat and let cool.
3. In a medium skillet over medium-low heat add ghee and carrots, cook slowly until carrots are very soft and cooked thoroughly. Add sugar and stir until sugar is dissolved, then add reduced milk and cook over low heat until milk is absorbed.
4. Serve immediately, garnish with cooked nuts and raisins.

DESSERTS

Coconut Barfi

Prep Time: 15 minutes

Servings: 4

Ingredients:

90g dried coconut
1 can sweetened condensed milk
1tsp vanilla extract
1tsp ginger, grated
1/8tsp cardamom
1/8tsp cinnamon
75g pistachios, chopped

Method:

1. Combine all ingredients, except the coconut, in a medium saucepan and cook for 3-4 minutes over medium-low heat, until the mixture comes together.
2. Remove from heat, cool and form into small bite sized balls and roll in coconut.
3. Cool completely in refrigerator and serve.

Plain Sweet Lassi

Prep Time: 5 minutes

Servings: 2

Ingredients:

500ml plain yogurt
Sugar to taste
2 cubes of ice

Method:

1. Combine all ingredients in a blender until sugar is dissolved. Serve immediately.

Printed in Great Britain
by Amazon.co.uk, Ltd.,
Marston Gate.